The Compliance Officer's HANDBOOK

Fourth Edition

Robert A. Wade, Esq. • Alex Krouse, JD, MHA

HCPro
a Simplify Compliance brand

The Compliance Officer's Handbook, Fourth Edition, is published by HCPro, a Simplify Compliance brand.

Download the additional materials of this book at *http://hcpro.com/downloads/13740*

ISBN: 978-1-64535-030-9
Product Code: CMPOH4

HCPro provides information resources for the healthcare industry.

Robert A. Wade, Esq., Author
Alex Krouse, JD, MHA, Author
Nicole Votta, Editor
Adrienne Trivers, Senior Manager, Product and Content
Matt Sharpe, Senior Manager, Creative Layout
AnnMarie Lemoine, Cover Designer

Arrangements can be made for quantity discounts. For more information, contact:

HCPro
100 Winners Circle, Suite 300
Brentwood, TN 37027
Telephone: 800-650-6787 or 781-639-1872
Fax: 800-639-8511
Email: *customerservice@hcpro.com*

Visit HCPro online at *www.hcpro.com* and *www.hcmarketplace.com*

Contents

Introduction

Our primary goal in creating this edition of *The Compliance Officer's Handbook* is to provide novice and experienced compliance officers with a trusted guide to the intricacies of healthcare compliance. In this book, you'll find detailed explanations, practice tools, and advice that will help you educate your organization about the importance of compliance and assist you in effectively managing real compliance issues.

Healthcare compliance touches every facet of the operation of a healthcare organization. Therefore, the more prepared you are in understanding these issues, the better you can serve your organization.

Above all, this book is meant to assist you and your organization in meeting compliance challenges and implementing an effective compliance program, while providing you with a practical approach to your role as a compliance officer.

The Challenges of Compliance

Compliance is challenging for individuals and organizations alike largely because the topic is expansive. Imagine, in healthcare organizations, that issues concerning insurance, health information, accreditation, practitioner licensing, fraud and abuse, and reimbursement are only the tip of the iceberg. Often, healthcare organizations are dealing with real estate issues and complex technologies and at the same time working toward being active participants in the communities they serve.

The federal regulations touching each of these issues are exhaustive and increasingly complex for organizations. The role of the compliance officer is to assist in implementing a program in which healthcare organizations can still reach their goals and broaden their services to the community, all while following the necessary rules and regulations to make that organization successful.

On a more individual level, working in compliance is challenging because of the expansive operations that exist within organizations. As mentioned above, healthcare organizations have multiple participants and issues of concern on more local levels. For example, the goals of practitioners such as physicians, nurse practitioners, and physician assistants may not align with the goals of federal regulations. Executives are often concerned with strategy for the organization as a whole whereas the legal staff may be concerned with individual legal issues that arise. However, each of these participants is required to remain compliant given these different goals or, at the very least, procedures to reach those goals.

The compliance officer or the compliance staff is the person or group assisting with this alignment. The primary goal should be to create a compliant organization; however, with competing goals and methods of reaching those goals, it can be tough to manage this process. Therefore, the organization itself is required to take responsibility for maintaining effective compliance programs.

Managers need to ensure that their individual departments are being compliant. Practitioners need to ensure that they can properly function while maintaining compliance. And executives need to be able to develop strategy with compliance in mind. The compliance staff is the group that acts as the traffic light: The staff can properly educate the various drivers of the rules. The staff can reprimand those who do not follow the rules. However, ultimately, those individuals need to take action on their own to remain compliant. This is the primary challenge for compliance officers and compliance staff.

How to Use This Book

Compliance has increasingly become an organizational component over the past 20 years largely due to the extensive and complicated federal regulations in the healthcare industry. These complex regulations create exposure for large healthcare delivery systems and small provider practices alike. This book is broken down into the essential topics to make you a more effective member of your organization and to allow your compliance program to be organized and implemented in an effective manner. The book is organized as follows:

Chapter 1: History and Evolution of Compliance

In this chapter, you will more fully understand the history of compliance and how compliance has become a necessary tool for both the government and for organizations themselves.

Chapter 2: OIG Guidance for Compliance Programs

The Office of Inspector General provides valuable information related to the proper operation and development of compliance programs. This chapter addresses those materials.

Chapter 3: Key Regulations for Compliance

Compliance officers deal with key laws and regulations in nearly all of their daily activities. This chapter focuses on the key areas on which compliance officers should focus, along with a brief explanation of those laws and regulations.

Chapter 4: Privacy and Security

With the proliferation of electronic health records and the constant exchange of patient data, privacy and security have become a necessary component of any compliance officer's daily activities. This section covers, in depth, many of the privacy and security issues that hospitals face.

Chapter 5: Revenue Cycle Compliance

All compliance programs should include processes targeted to the revenue cycle, including coding, billing, and reimbursement. This chapter discusses how the revenue cycle operates, risk areas, and strategies to mitigate risk.

Chapter 6: Fair Market Value and Commercial Reasonableness

Fair market value considerations relate to many if not all of the relationships that hospitals have with physicians. A compliance officer should be well versed on the matter. This chapter provides a detailed understanding of fair market value.

Chapter 7: Internal Strategies for Best Practices

Developing best practices for compliance requires specific internal strategies. This chapter focuses on how developing best practices and developing internal strategies go hand in hand. The practical strategies provided in this chapter will help compliance officers develop strategies for their own organizations. This chapter also details best practices on how to structure the compliance department and how the compliance function relates to other hospital departments, executive leadership, and the board.

Chapter 8: The Risk Assessment

Understanding risk is an important element of a compliance officer's job. Performing a risk assessment provides you and your organization with an advanced understanding of risk. This chapter provides a detailed plan for developing your own risk assessment.

Chapter 9: Training Strategies

Compliance programs are most effective when the staff and organization as a whole take an ownership interest in compliance. This chapter focuses on important training methods to build a culture of compliance within your organization.

Chapter 10: Monitoring and Auditing

A compliance officer must routinely monitor and audit various areas within the hospital or healthcare organization to ensure compliance. This chapter provides the practical tips for implementing monitoring and auditing programs.

Chapter 11: Effective Internal Investigations

Internal investigations are important because they not only assist the organization in strengthening the compliance program but they also help ensure that the organization is willing and able to maintain compliance. This chapter will give you the tools and knowledge to manage an effective internal investigation.

The chapters in this book will provide you, your staff, and your organization with a strong understanding of the history of compliance and the current issues facing hospitals on a daily basis. The information will help compliance officers and compliance staff develop internal strategies, risk assessments, monitoring plans, and the knowledge to effectively manage an internal investigation. Above all, the information in this book is both practical and timely, and it will assist you in the daily compliance challenges that your organization faces.

In addition to the practical information found in the chapters, the book also includes many forms and documents that may be used on a daily basis in compliance offices. Many of the forms were drafted specifically so compliance officers could use them within their own organizations. You will find downloadable versions of these tools at the HCPro website address listed on the copyright page at the beginning of this book.

About the Authors

Robert A. Wade, Esq.

Robert A. Wade, Esq., is a partner in the law firm of Barnes & Thornburg LLP. He concentrates his practice on representing healthcare clients, including large health systems, hospitals, ambulatory surgical centers, physician groups, physicians, and other medical providers. Wade's expertise includes representing clients with respect to the Stark Act, Anti-Kickback Statute, False Claims Act, and Emergency Medical Treatment and Active Labor Act of 1986.

Wade is nationally recognized in all aspects of healthcare compliance, including developing, monitoring, and documentation of an effective compliance program. He has experience in representing healthcare clients with respect to issues being investigated by the Department of Justice and the Office of Inspector General and experience negotiating and implementing corporate integrity agreements. His expertise includes assisting clients in documenting and defending financial arrangements between healthcare providers, including referring physicians, as being fair market value and commercially reasonable. He has operationally practical experience, having served as a general counsel and organizational integrity officer for a multihospital system for six and a half years.

Wade is also the creator of Captain Integrity (*www.captainintegrity.com*), a unique compliance program branding and education resource that has received national recognition and has been used by many hospitals, health systems, and other providers.

Alex Krouse, JD, MHA

Alex Krouse, JD, MHA, is an attorney with extensive experience in healthcare operations specific to provider alignment initiatives. He provides advice to health systems on new healthcare initiatives, effective utilization of healthcare professionals, and strategic provider alignment. This includes addressing significant business and legal issues, ranging from the Stark Law to Medicare reimbursement regulations. In addition to his experience in healthcare operations and strategy, Krouse is a national thought leader in provider compensation strategy, including fair market value. He serves on multiple national committees focused on provider compensation and writes and speaks extensively on fraud and abuse issues and emerging regulatory issues. Prior to practicing law, Krouse gained experience in hospital operations both in a large health system and in a community hospital.

Chapter 1

History and Evolution of Compliance

Welcome to healthcare compliance!

It is no easy task to comply with all the legal requirements that govern the practice of medicine, including statutes, rules, regulations, and policies set by the government, insurance programs, and payers. But to participate in any governmental health insurance program, a provider must do exactly that—maintain corporate compliance. To aid you in reaching that goal, this book will provide practical and operationally sensitive guidance to assist in identifying and preventing potential problems; it will also provide recommendations on what to do if problems are found.

Due to the complex regulatory and third-party payer requirements, compliance issues will arise in every healthcare entity. Many regulations and requirements necessitate different responses. By way of example, physician supervision or medical record documentation requirements may differ from the requirements of third-party payers. The goal of an effective compliance program is to understand risk areas, test risk areas, and take corrective actions when necessary.

Your organization has implemented a corporate compliance program because it is committed to identifying and preventing potential problems. "Corporate compliance" refers to your organization's pledge to operate within the statutes, rules, regulations, and policies set by the government, insurance programs, and payers.

The Office of Inspector General (OIG) of the U.S. Department of Health and Human Services (HHS) has issued model compliance guidance in addition to an annual document called a *Work Plan* that outlines the focus areas related to fraud and abuse by medical providers. The model guidance and *Work Plan* cover all healthcare sectors. To make sense of this guidance, you must first understand why the OIG has recommended compliance programs for the healthcare industry.

The History of Compliance

Compliance is not a new notion. Its history reaches back to the 1860s, during the Civil War era, when the False Claims Act (FCA) was passed to prevent profiteers from selling bogus goods to the Union Army. Amended several times since, this act mandates fines and penalties of triple the value of each false claim made against a government agency. At first glance, it may not seem clear how a law created to protect the government in wartime has anything to do with healthcare practices. However, the FCA has in fact become a powerful weapon against fraudulent claims issued by healthcare providers or fraudulent activities conducted by healthcare providers who receive governmental funding (such as to support research).

In 1996, the Health Insurance Portability and Accountability Act (HIPAA) authorized the creation of the Medicare Integrity Program. This program directed federal agencies (including HHS, the Department of Justice [DOJ], and the Department of Labor) to develop an array of tools to combat fraudulent claims and abusive practices of healthcare providers. For the purposes of governmental interpretation, "fraud" is a deliberate act intended to obtain improper payment, and "abuse" is a repeated act that may not be deliberate but that nevertheless results in improper payment.

FIGURE 1.1

What Is Fraud?	What Is Abuse?
• Crimes of guile and deceit • Intentional and material false statements or representations made to obtain some benefit to which one is not entitled • Intentionally retaining monies received from the government that the provider later learns it is not entitled to retain • Reckless disregard for compliance with statutes, rules, and regulations • Violations that occur when actions are committed for oneself or on behalf of another party • Acts performed knowingly, willfully, and intentionally • Violations that warrant criminal, civil, or administrative action • Civil fraud, which has a lower standard of proof and lesser penalties than criminal fraud	• Practices resulting, directly or indirectly, in unnecessary increased costs • Overuse of medical services, products, or both • Medically unnecessary services or products • Failure to conform to professionally recognized codes or standards • Unfair and unreasonable pricing • Restrictions of patient choice • Restrictions of competition • Failure to provide quality services • Failure to provide services/supplies billed • Financially enticing beneficiaries to receive service from specific providers/suppliers

The OIG goes to great lengths to assert that it intends to take action against providers who commit deliberate acts of fraud. It states that providers aren't subject to penalties for innocent errors but for offenses committed with actual knowledge, reckless disregard, or deliberate ignorance of the falsity of the claims. However, the OIG also notes that providers and their staff members must commit sufficient resources and use auditing and monitoring programs to ensure that the claims they file are accurate, reasonable, necessary, and consistent with billing documentation and grant/funding requirements.

Amendments to HIPAA further strengthened the program in 1997, and additional regulations were added under the Balanced Budget Act of 1998 and the Balanced Budget Relief Act of 1999. These acts were not the first to regulate healthcare, but they were the first to use the broad and far-reaching powers of the FCA in the healthcare industry. Further, under the Patient Protection and Affordable Care Act (ACA), the government has increased resources to combat healthcare fraud, waste, and abuse. The ACA provided increased sentencing for fraud and abuse in excess of $1,000,000, increased use of predictive modeling technology to identify inappropriate claims, and allocated an additional $350,000,000 to the Medicare Integrity Program over 10 years to increase fraud and abuse investigations. New initiatives are implemented every year. The government has consistently recovered more money from settlements and judgments than what it spends on various auditing/review initiatives.

What brought these actions about? A combination of factors persuaded Congress, federal agencies, and the American public that the economics of U.S. healthcare delivery could be improved. The first of these factors was the cost of improved and necessary technology. As the industry discovered more and more technical means to improve care, public demand for the newest and best technological innovations increased—and so, despite the increased cost of these new diagnosis methods, healthcare providers began to use them.

The associated costs of new equipment were inevitably passed on to patients, health insurers, and federal reimbursement programs as healthcare providers approved the technology for Medicare and Medicaid reimbursement. As physicians' diagnoses improved, so did patient outcomes. However, the cost of care also increased.

The American public objected to this increase, which was evident in the steady rise of their out-of-pocket expenses. Health insurers and managed care companies passed as much cost along to patients and program beneficiaries as possible through increased premiums, copayments, and deductibles. Many Americans found these higher costs unmanageable, and private citizens and employers began to drop or limit health insurance coverage. Managed care insurers tried to cut costs by limiting treatment options, but this tactic was increasingly challenged by physicians who were unwilling to potentially compromise their quality of care.

As advances in medicine increased life spans, Medicare and state Medicaid actuaries became increasingly aware of the longevity and number of recipients accessing these programs. The enrollment age of 65 has not changed since the inception of the Medicare program, even though the average length of life has steadily increased. The architects of the Medicare and Medicaid programs likely did not anticipate the sheer number of senior citizens now enrolling.

In addition, there was increasing evidence of deliberate acts of fraud on the part of some unscrupulous healthcare providers. Under the complex prospective payment system, Maximum Allowable and Acceptable Charge schedules, and the Resource-Based Relative Value Scale system used by Medicare, as well as various entitlement programs used by state Medicaid programs, some providers deliberately selected billing practices that maximized the reimbursement obtained through these programs. In some cases, financial experts theorize that in order to maximize payment, hospitals, specialty care programs, and physicians may have intentionally classified basic services as more complex, or billed for services that were not rendered at all or that were not medically necessary.

Many healthcare practices created programs (such as imaging services within physician practices) and even entire facilities (such as long-term acute care hospitals, ambulatory surgery centers, and freestanding imaging centers) to obtain reimbursement from specialized services. These programs and actions placed additional strain on the Medicare Trust Fund, a fund already stretched by increasing numbers of beneficiaries and covered procedures.

In an effort to reduce fraud and abuse, Congress in 1996 passed HIPAA, a far-reaching statute that has affected every aspect of healthcare delivery. In addition to helping employees transfer their health insurance coverage from job to job, HIPAA provided for fraud and abuse investigation of healthcare organizations, established a new payment mechanism for hospital outpatient services, and allowed for other extensive changes in business practices and regulation for care providers.

With funding ensured by HIPAA through establishment of the Medicare Integrity Program, federal agencies began to gear up to conduct extensive fraud and abuse investigations. Hospitals and affiliated large academic physician practices were a natural first target, due to their size and the thousands of complex services and procedures they billed for each year. Investigators targeted obvious examples of fraudulent activity and rapidly opened cases against major hospital corporations, drug and device manufacturers, and physician practices. Settlements have resulted in the government collecting more than it spends on investigations. Simply stated, the funding of investigations has generated a good return on the monies invested.

In fiscal year 2018, the DOJ announced that they recovered $2.8 billion under cases involving the False Claims Act (FCA) (DOJ, 2018). "Of the $2.8 billion in settlements and judgments recovered by the Department of Justice this past fiscal year [fiscal year 2018], $2.5 billion involved the healthcare industry, including drug and medical device manufacturers, managed care providers, hospitals, pharmacies, hospice organizations, laboratories, and physicians." In a press release, the DOJ stated that this "is the ninth consecutive year that the Department's civil health care fraud settlements and judgments have exceeded $2 billion. The recoveries included in the $2.5 billion reflect only federal losses but, in many of these cases, the Department was instrumental in recovering additional millions of dollars for state Medicaid programs" (DOJ, 2018). Based upon the DOJ's continued success in using the FCA, the healthcare industry remains a significant target.

The press release further stated that the "[d]epartment continued its commitment to use the False Claims Act and other civil remedies to deter and redress fraud by individuals as well as corporations. For example, after a two-week jury trial, the Department obtained judgments totaling more than $114 million against three individuals who were found to have paid physicians illegal remuneration disguised as 'handling fees' of between $10 and $17 for each patient they referred to two blood testing laboratories: Health Diagnostic Laboratories of Richmond, Virginia ('HDL'), and Singulex Inc., of Alameda, California ('Singulex'). The government also introduced evidence at trial that this kickback scheme resulted in physicians referring patients to HDL and Signulex for medically unnecessary tests which were then billed to federal healthcare programs." The press release went on to enumerate additional examples of individual accountability under the FCA.

The majority of the government's recoveries involved *qui tam* whistleblowers. In the 2018 press release, the DOJ stated that, of the settlements and judgments during fiscal year 2018, "over $2.1 billion arose from lawsuits filed under the *qui tam* provisions of the False Claims Act. During the same period, the government paid out

$301 million to the individuals who exposed fraud and false claims by filing these actions." Assistant Attorney General Jody Hunt stated that "whistleblowers have played a vital role in unmasking fraudulent schemes that might otherwise evade detection." The press release continued to quote Hunt by stating that "[t]he taxpayers owe a debt of gratitude to those who often put much on the line to expose such schemes."

State Medicaid Fraud Control Units (MFCU) recovered $1.8 billion during fiscal year 2017. According to the OIG's Medicaid Fraud Control Units Fiscal Year 2017 Annual Report, MFCUs obtained 1,528 criminal convictions, excluded 1,181 individuals or entities from participating in federally funded healthcare programs, obtained 961 civil settlements and judgments, and recovered $693 million in criminal and $1.1 billion in civil recoveries. For every dollar spent by MFCUs on costs and expenses associated with cases, the MFCUs recovered $6.52. Of the 1,528 criminal convictions, 371 criminal convictions involved patient abuse and neglect. Such recoveries, consistent with the recoveries by the DOJ under the False Claims Act, covered all types of providers, including physicians and nonphysician practitioners (OIG, 2018).

On the heels of widely publicized reports of fraud in the 1960s and 1970s, the defense industry mandated that contracting companies institute corporate compliance and integrity programs. Following this example, the OIG became convinced that voluntary compliance programs were the most effective means of addressing fraud among healthcare providers. The OIG has issued compliance program guidance for numerous types of care providers, including home health agencies, durable medical equipment suppliers, nursing facilities, hospitals, laboratories, third-party billing companies, pharmaceutical manufacturers, ambulance suppliers, and physician practices. In part, these documents aim to lead providers toward development of what federal investigators will consider effective fraud prevention programs. Although the OIG has not mandated adherence with all guidance requirements, the guidance provides a good road map for the development of an effective compliance program.

The typical guidance found in these documents is structured and offers a very broad overview of what a compliance program may incorporate. Some have rightfully noted that the guidance is voluntary, not mandatory. However, because the OIG is the agency that usually investigates potential healthcare fraud and abuse (and because it may recommend further investigation by agencies such as the DOJ), adopting its guidance as part of your organization's compliance plan can help providers avoid trouble and act as an important negotiating point if an organization is investigated or self-reports an issue. Implementing applicable compliance guidance as part of your organization's compliance plan can also assist in the event of a *qui tam* case/allegation.

Why Is Compliance Important?

A compliance program may help to lower your organization's potential liability for errors—such as inaccurate coding or incorrect billing—after the claim has been billed or the reimbursement has been received.

By voluntarily implementing a compliance program, an organization may do the following:

- Demonstrate its commitment to honest and responsible corporate conduct
- Increase the likelihood of preventing, identifying, and correcting unlawful and unethical behavior at an early stage
- Encourage employees to report potential problems to allow for appropriate internal inquiry and corrective action
- Minimize any financial loss to the government and taxpayers, as well as any corresponding financial loss to the facility, through early detection and reporting
- Protect its reputation
- Improve morale

Risks of noncompliance

Healthcare organizations that are not in compliance with certain government rules and regulations may face harsh penalties that could result in monetary settlements, mandated compliance programs (through corporate integrity or certification of compliance agreements with the government), exclusion from government-sponsored programs (such as Medicare and Medicaid), and possible criminal prosecution and incarceration for intentional and egregious acts.

Organizations suspected of fraud or abuse must deal with targeted government audits, reviews, and interviews of employees. These investigations usually result in hefty legal expenses for the provider, the potential for a costly civil monetary settlement, negative public perception, and a general disruption of operations. As noted earlier, if organizations are found by the OIG to have consistently failed to comply with a regulation or law, they will most likely have to negotiate and operate under a corporate integrity agreement, which is a government-designed and mandated compliance program, to continue participating in government-sponsored healthcare programs. These agreements, which can be onerous and costly, strive to hold the organization accountable for implementing compliance programs with OIG oversight.

As a compliance officer, your goal should be to develop a compliance program that identifies problems so that they can be fixed proactively, thus ensuring that your organization never has the need for a corporate integrity agreement.

Solvency of the Medicare Trust Fund

To understand the need for compliance activities in the healthcare industry, one only needs to look at the financial viability of the Medicare Trust Fund. The financial outlook for Medicare continues to raise concerns, with total expenditures anticipated to increase faster than workers' earnings or the overall economy.

In the 2018 Annual Report of the Boards of Trustees of the Federal Hospital Insurance and Federal Supplementary Medical Insurance Trust Funds, the trustees projected that the Medicare Trust Fund would remain solvent until 2026, three years earlier than their 2017 projection, which placed the insolvency date at 2029 (CMS, 2018). Because of the continued deterioration, there is concern that the Medicare Trust Fund will become insolvent unless drastic changes are made.

There are five significant methods available to protect the Medicare Trust Fund:

1. Economic growth that results in increased income and Medicare revenue
2. Aggressive efforts to fight waste, fraud, and abuse
3. Changes in payments and/or payment methodology
4. Changes in coverage (both eligibility [i.e., age of coverage] and services/procedures)
5. Increased taxes

Policies and Procedures

Policies and procedures are critical components of any compliance program. The OIG's 1998 *Compliance Program Guidance for Hospitals* states that one of the seven elements of a comprehensive compliance program should be "the development and distribution of written standards of conduct as well as written policies and procedures that promote the hospital's commitment to compliance and that addresses specific areas of potential fraud, such as claim development and submission processes, code gaming and financial relationships with physicians and other healthcare professionals."

The guidance further states that "every compliance program should require the distribution of written compliance policies that identify specific areas of risk to the hospital. These policies should be developed under the direction and supervision of the chief compliance officer and compliance committee, and, at a minimum, should be provided to all individuals who are affected by the particular policy at issue, including the hospital's agents and independent contractors."

Compliance Beyond Medicare and Medicaid Fraud

Without a doubt, compliance officers in the healthcare sector initially spent an overwhelming—but necessary—amount of time on Medicare/Medicaid fraud issues. Most hospitals formed compliance departments as a result of the antifraud initiatives taken by the OIG and the DOJ.

Although these issues are important, compliance involves more than Medicare/Medicaid fraud. The compliance department's role is to assist the institution in complying with all laws, including employment laws, environmental laws, antitrust laws, and tax-exempt status protection for tax-exempt organizations.

In many other industries, antitrust laws are a standard compliance concern. However, in healthcare, antitrust issues continue to take center stage. This fact is well documented in the March 2013 report of the Federal Trade Commission (FTC)'s *Overview of FTC Antitrust Actions in Health Care Services and Products.* In its 199-page overview, the FTC describes the actions and activities of its Health Care Division, which touched all sectors of the healthcare industry, including pharmaceutical and device manufacturers, hospitals, and physician groups. The federal government, state attorneys general, and private parties each have a role in antitrust law enforcement. Compliance officers must deal specifically with two federal agencies that enforce the antitrust laws: the DOJ and the FTC.

These two agencies cooperate by releasing joint policy statements, such as the *Horizontal Merger Guidelines,* the *Guidelines on Collaborations Among Competitors,* and the *Statements on Antitrust Enforcement in Health Care.* These guidelines are not law, but antitrust enforcement agencies use them extensively when evaluating the antitrust implications of a healthcare transaction. The Sherman Antitrust Act and the Clayton Antitrust Act are the core antitrust statutes.

Sherman Antitrust Act

The Sherman Antitrust Act consists of two provisions: Section 1 (conspiracies in restraint of trade) and Section 2 (monopolies).

Section 1: Conspiracies in restraint of trade

This section prohibits "contracts, combinations, and conspiracies" in restraint of trade. However, the courts interpret this section as applying only to agreements that "substantially" restrain trade. For this to be the case, two or more parties capable of conspiring must have reached an agreement that substantially restrains trade.

To evaluate a Section 1 claim, find out whether there are two separate economic entities and whether the entities are acting on their own behalf or are acting as "one economic entity." For example, the following parties are typically acting as one economic entity:

- Parent and subsidiary corporations
- A hospital and its collective medical staff
- Corporations and their employees

The next question is whether the agreement represents a substantial restraint of trade. The courts have determined that certain actions, such as price fixing, market allocation agreements, and various types of boycotts, are so clearly anticompetitive that they automatically violate antitrust laws. Under this scenario (called the "per se" analysis), defendants cannot offer any justification for the conduct.

For other agreements that do not fall into the "per se" category, the "rule of reason" applies. Under this rule, the court, after hearing the entities' procompetitive justifications, considers whether the activity as a whole substantially affects competition.

These cases often center on complex market definition issues and seek answers as to whether the defendants have "market power" to injure the competitive process. The court must analyze the product and geographic components of the market. The product market represents the item or service at issue. It includes the service and its reasonable substitutes. In the geographic market analysis, the court questions how far consumers are willing to go for substitute services.

Often, antitrust cases under the "rule of reason" are won or lost depending on the product and geographic market definition issues. Under the "rule of reason," defendants may offer justification for their conduct. Because healthcare is perceived as being a local issue, the geographic market may not be very large.

Section 2: Monopolies

This section of the Sherman Antitrust Act prohibits organizations from illegally forming or maintaining monopolies. Monopolies are not illegal if organizations form them as the result of historic patterns, due to superior products, or by accident. Nevertheless, for this rule to apply, only one organization has to be involved. Under this section, organizations are also prohibited from attempting or conspiring to monopolize. In general, it is more difficult for the government to prove monopolization than it is to prove that an organization violated Section 1.

Clayton Antitrust Act

Antitrust enforcers heavily use Section 7 of the Clayton Antitrust Act. This section governs mergers. Many of the fundamental antitrust principles apply, such as defining the relevant product and geographic markets.

Section 7 examines whether a merger is likely to "substantially lessen competition or tend to create a monopoly." It focuses on predictions and is not bound by the current status of the competitive market.

Who Polices Corporate Compliance?

Government agencies and government-hired contractors, which are well funded and have substantial claims databases, are on the lookout for outliers and instances of provider noncompliance. Through the years, they have become more aggressive in identifying and investigating potential errors and negotiating settlements.

The following is a list of the major players in healthcare compliance enforcement:

- *The OIG.* The OIG is the primary investigative and enforcement arm of HHS. OIG agents and lawyers investigate and prosecute violators for suspected healthcare fraud and abuse and, when warranted, negotiate corporate integrity agreements. In addition, the agency provides compliance education and guidance to the industry.
- *Centers for Medicare & Medicaid Services (CMS).* CMS is recognized primarily for its rulemaking authority. However, because CMS is also responsible for Medicare, it has contracted private organizations to review Medicare claims. These contractors, called carriers and fiscal intermediaries, look for outliers and abnormalities that might result in refunds of overpayments.
- *The DOJ and U.S. Attorneys' Offices.* The DOJ civilly and criminally prosecutes organizations for healthcare fraud and abuse, often under the Anti-Kickback Statute, the Physician Self-Referral Law (Stark), and the FCA. These investigations often result in civil settlements and criminal indictments, which frequently involve incarceration.
- *The FBI.* The FBI assists the DOJ and the OIG by investigating suspected healthcare fraud. Healthcare fraud is an enforcement priority, and its investigation is well funded under HIPAA.
- *State MFCUs.* Medicaid fraud units use the techniques devised by the federal agencies to spot possible fraud and abuse in state Medicaid programs. They often partner with federal law enforcement to make fraud cases. State MFCUs are expanding their efforts to investigate fraud issues.
- *The Office for Civil Rights (OCR).* The OCR is the HHS arm that investigates breach notifications and alleged violations of the patient health information Privacy and Security rules within HIPAA.
- *Private payers.* Private payers establish security units or divisions to investigate fraud within or against their health plans.

- *Qui tam litigants.* Any individual, including employees, can, under the FCA, bring a fraud complaint on behalf of the government in federal district court.

High-Risk Practices

Government agencies, along with fiscal intermediaries, are on the lookout for billing activity that could indicate fraud or abuse. The following are common practices that would lead to government scrutiny.

Upcoding

Upcoding involves using a higher-paying billing code rather than the code that actually reflects services furnished to a patient. It can range from a physician claiming a higher-level evaluation and management service than he or she rendered to elaborate schemes wherein entire sets of services are coded inappropriately. In the hospital setting, the focus is on code pairs (known as diagnosis-related groups) for similar medical conditions, with one pair resulting in a higher reimbursement depending on the condition of the patient and the level of services provided.

Billing for services not rendered

This involves submitting a claim representing that the provider performed a service when the provider did not actually perform all or part of that service.

Billing for medically unnecessary services

Such billing involves claims that intentionally seek reimbursement for services not warranted by the patient's current and documented medical condition. Providers should bill only for services that meet Medicare's "reasonable and necessary" standard.

Duplicate billing

Duplicate billing is submitting more than one claim for the same service or submitting bills to more than one primary payer at the same time.

Unbundling

Medicare requires organizations to bill certain tests and procedures together, providing a single reduced reimbursement for the bundle. Unbundling is the practice of submitting such bills in fragments to maximize reimbursement.

Kickbacks

Kickbacks involve offering anything of value, in cash or in kind, with the intent to induce referrals.

Improper place of service codes

Place of service codes are two-digit codes established by CMS that represent the setting in which a medical service was provided. For example, place of service code 11 represents that a service was performed in a physician's office, whereas place of service code 22 represents that the service was performed in an outpatient hospital department. Improper use of these codes can result in overpayment.

Physician financial arrangements with designated health service entities

All financial arrangements between physicians (and their family members) and designated health service entities (e.g., hospitals) must meet all components of a Stark Law exception; if they do not, the physician cannot refer to the entity, and the entity cannot bill for services rendered from the tainted referral. All such arrangements must be both fair market value and commercially reasonable.

Steps Toward Compliance

Your involvement can help improve your organization's culture of compliance. Here are some simple things you can do:

- Learn and be able to articulate the ways in which your job is critical to the organization's compliance efforts. Consider how errors or lack of training could put the organization in jeopardy.
- Be involved with executive leadership and the governing body. Attend meetings and be involved in email communications where compliance issues may arise.
- Be available and approachable so issues and concerns can be brought to your attention.
- Be willing to take extra steps concerning your compliance duties—ask hard questions and, when in doubt, double-check policies or seek outside assistance from knowledgeable healthcare attorneys or consultants.
- Act and inquire in accordance with the concepts expressed in your organization's code of conduct.
- Feel free to raise issues with supervisors or managers informally or by using more formal reporting mechanisms (e.g., hotlines). It is better to ask questions and raise issues than to leave matters unresolved.
- View compliance as an opportunity rather than as a burden; consider it a critical component of your organization's overall quality improvement process.
- Actively request and seek training and education when needed.
- Regard auditing and monitoring findings as opportunities for improvement.
- Take the time to study new policies or procedures as they arise, and incorporate them into your job and the jobs of those affected. If you are confused, ask questions and be flexible.
- Seek timely closure of issues. Notify compliance reporters regarding the closure of the investigation and the corrective actions implemented.

- Work collaboratively with the organization on compliance oversight and issues.
- Monitor how compliance is discussed by executive leadership and the governing body.

References

Centers for Medicare & Medicaid Services (CMS). (2018). 2018 Annual Report of the Boards of Trustees of the Federal Hospital Insurance and Federal Supplementary Medical Insurance Trust Funds. https://www.cms.gov/Research-Statistics-Data-and-Systems/Statistics-Trends-and-Reports/ReportsTrustFunds/Downloads/TR2018.pdf

Department of Justice (DOJ). (2018). Justice Department recovers over $2.8 billion from False Claims Act cases in fiscal year 2018. https://www.justice.gov/opa/pr/justice-department-recovers-over-28-billion-false-claims-act-cases-fiscal-year-2018

Office of Inspector General (OIG). (2018). Medicaid Fraud Control Units fiscal year 2017 annual report. https://oig.hhs.gov/oei/reports/oei-09-18-00180.pdf

Chapter 2
OIG Guidance for Compliance Programs

The Office of Inspector General (OIG) believes that an effective compliance program is a sound investment for providers. With the increased complexity of integrated delivery systems, it is useful to understand that guidance from the OIG has been directed to various segments of the healthcare industry. In this chapter, we will cover the OIG's *Compliance Program Guidance for Hospitals,* provide an overview of the OIG's suggestions, and explain how to implement them.

Compliance Program Guidance for Hospitals

The OIG issues an annual *Work Plan* that describes the various projects on which the Office of Audit Services, Office of Evaluation and Inspections, Office of Investigations, and Office of Counsel to the Inspector General will focus their attention in the upcoming year. The *Work Plan* includes projects planned in each of the department's major entities: Centers for Medicare & Medicaid Services (CMS), the public health agencies, and the Administrations for Children, Families, and Aging. Visit *http://oig.hhs.gov/reports-and-publications/workplan/index.asp* for information on the most recent *Work Plan*. In more recent years, the OIG has issued an annual plan that is updated on a monthly basis. The agency also releases a list of Active *Work Plan* Items. Organizations can use these resources to focus their compliance efforts.

The OIG first published compliance guidance in 1998 and a supplemental guidance in 2005. The initial guidance and all subsequent compliance publications are intended to help reduce fraud and abuse. Today, the OIG continues that aim and includes guidelines for hospitals as for well as a wide variety of healthcare organizations that serve beneficiaries of Medicare, Medicaid, and other federal healthcare programs. The goal of these documents is to establish behaviors that promote a higher level of ethics and compliance in the healthcare industry.

The OIG works with CMS, the Department of Justice (DOJ), and various other sectors of the healthcare community to develop these guidelines. Although they are voluntary, they are considered industry best practices, so it is strongly recommended that hospitals implement the applicable recommendations.

Compliance Program Guidance for Other Healthcare Sectors

In addition, the *Work Plan* contains information relevant to other healthcare entities beyond hospitals. The information can help healthcare entities understand the focus areas for the year. The OIG also publishes compliance guidance for other healthcare entities, including nursing facilities, pharmaceutical manufacturers, small group physician practices, third-party billing companies, and many more. These documents provide a focused guide for those types of entities in promoting compliance in their respective industries. As hospitals and health systems have expanded and diversified the services they offer, many of these documents may be pertinent to them despite not having been specifically written for them. Therefore, to ensure that your compliance plan is consistent with your organization's services, these are ideal resources for development of a broad compliance program.

Compliance program elements

The OIG's compliance program elements are intended to guide entities, whether small or large, urban or rural, for-profit or nonprofit. Every entity can benefit from these guidelines, and they can—and should—be adjusted to fit the needs of individual entities.

The OIG says that a solid compliance program should include the ability to do the following:

- Concretely demonstrate to employees and to the community at large the entity's strong commitment to honest and responsible provider and corporate conduct
- Provide a more accurate view of employee and contractor behavior relating to fraud and abuse
- Identify and prevent criminal and unethical conduct
- Tailor itself to the entity's specific needs
- Improve the quality of patient care
- Create a centralized source of information on healthcare statutes, regulations, and other program directives related to fraud and abuse and associated issues
- Develop a methodology that encourages employees to report potential problems
- Develop procedures that allow for prompt, thorough investigation of alleged misconduct by corporate officers, managers, employees, independent contractors, physicians, other healthcare professionals, and consultants
- Initiate immediate and appropriate corrective action
- Minimize government loss due to incorrect reimbursement through early detection and reporting, thereby reducing the entity's exposure to civil damages and penalties, criminal sanctions, and administrative remedies such as program exclusion

According to the OIG, comprehensive compliance programs should include the following seven elements:

1. Standards and procedures. Organizations should develop and distribute written standards of conduct as well as written policies and procedures that promote the entity's commitment to compliance (e.g., by including adherence to compliance as an element in evaluating managers and employees) and that address specific areas of potential fraud, such as claims development and submission processes, code gaming, and financial relationships with physicians and other healthcare professionals.
2. Designation of a compliance officer. Organizations should choose a person in a high-level position who has direct access to senior management and the board to serve as chief compliance officer. This person will receive support from a compliance committee. The compliance officer should be charged with the responsibility of operating and monitoring the compliance program and should report directly to the CEO and the governing body. The compliance officer must feel comfortable making potentially unpopular decisions and recommendations.
3. Appropriate training and education. Organizations should develop regular, effective education and training programs for all affected employees so that they are fully capable of executing their role in compliance with rules, regulations, and other standards. The education should include the elements of the provider's compliance program and job-specific compliance requirements.
4. Open lines of communication. Organizations should set up an anonymous reporting mechanism (e.g., a hotline) to help receive complaints and respond to compliance problems. Organizations also should adopt procedures to protect the anonymity of complainants and to protect whistleblowers from retaliation.
5. Response to detected problems. Organizations should develop a system to respond to allegations of improper/illegal activities and enforce appropriate disciplinary action against employees who have violated internal compliance policies, applicable statutes, regulations, or federal healthcare program requirements.
6. Internal auditing and monitoring. Organizations should develop detailed annual audit plans to minimize the exposures associated with improper claims and billing practices. The use of audits or other evaluation techniques should help reduce identified problem areas.
7. Enforcement of disciplinary standards. Organizations should promote and enforce their compliance program consistently and through appropriate incentives. Those who engage in misconduct or who fail to take reasonable steps to prevent, detect, or report misconduct should be subject to discipline.

The OIG's Risk Areas

The OIG risk areas are constantly changing. Although we will identify areas of special risk later in this chapter, it is important to note that some risk areas are very specific. For example, in 2020, the OIG specifically intends to review overprescribing in the Appalachian region. Other risk areas are broader. As an example, in 2020, the OIG intends to compare and analyze provider-based clinics vs. freestanding clinics. This issue impacts organizations across the country. Compliance officers must be cognizant of both specific and broad risk areas, understand the risks, and actively address them as they arise in the OIG's *Work Plan*.

The following areas are identified by the OIG as being of special concern:

- Provider-based status requirements. The provider-based status allows another facility to bill as a part of the main provider. This normally occurs by the use of hospital-owned physician practices. Provider-based status can result in additional Medicare payments.
- Medicare transfer policy coding errors. Under 42 *CFR* §412.4(e), a hospital discharging a patient is paid the full diagnosis-related group (DRG) amount, whereas if a transfer occurs, the payment is a graduated per diem rate that does not exceed the full DRG payment. The primary concern is whether hospitals are coding as discharges patients who should actually be coded as transfers.
- Billing for items or services not actually rendered. Doing so involves submitting a claim for a service that was not performed.
- Providing medically unnecessary services. As defined by the OIG, a claim requesting payment for medically unnecessary services intentionally seeks reimbursement for a service not warranted by the patient's current and documented medical condition. For further explanation, see 42 USC 1395y(a)(1)(A) ("no payment may be made under part A or part B for any expenses incurred for items or services which ... are not reasonable and necessary for the diagnosis or treatment of illness or injury or to improve the functioning of the malformed body member").
- Upcoding. This is the practice of using a billing code that provides a higher payment rate than the billing code that actually reflects the service furnished to the patient. The OIG has made upcoding a major focus of its enforcement efforts.
- Diagnosis-related group (DRG) creep. Like upcoding, DRG creep is the practice of billing using a DRG code that provides a higher payment rate than the one that accurately reflects the service furnished to the patient.
- Outpatient services rendered in connection with inpatient stays. This problem involves duplicate claims—specifically, the submission of claims for nonphysician outpatient services that were already included in the hospital's inpatient payment under the prospective payment system.
- Teaching physician and resident requirements for teaching hospitals. Hospitals need to monitor the services rendered by residents and ensure appropriate involvement and oversight by teaching physicians.

- Duplicate billing. This occurs when the hospital submits more than one claim for the same service or when a bill is submitted to more than one primary payer at the same time. Organizations must take care to bill carefully and promptly refund any overpayments. Duplicate billing can occur due to simple errors, but repeated double billing could be viewed as a false claim by the OIG.
- False cost reports. The submission of false cost reports is usually limited to certain Part A providers, such as hospitals, skilled nursing facilities, and home health agencies, which are reimbursed in part based on their self-reported operating costs. Only allowable costs should be included on cost reports.
- Unbundling. This is the practice of submitting bills in pieces to maximize the reimbursement for various tests or procedures that are required to be billed together and, therefore, at a reduced cost.
- Patients' freedom of choice. This involves hospital discharge planners referring patients to home health agencies, durable medical equipment suppliers, or long-term care and rehabilitation providers. Patients should be provided with a choice of postdischarge providers.
- Failure to refund credit balances. Providers are required to monitor payments received in error (e.g., credit balances) and implement a process to refund such payments.
- Hospital incentives that violate the Anti-Kickback Statute. Practices that may violate the Anti-Kickback Statute or other similar federal regulations include excessive payment for medical directorships, free or below-fair-market-value rents or fees for administrative duties, interest-free loans, and excessive payment for intangible assets in physician practice acquisitions.
- Joint ventures. Such arrangements are typically established between physicians and those providing items or services paid for by a federal healthcare program (e.g., Medicare), which may violate the Anti-Kickback Statute.
- Stark Law (physician self-referral). If an entity bills or performs designated health services, such as inpatient or outpatient hospital services, laboratory services, or radiology services, all financial arrangements between such entities and referring physicians must meet all components of an applicable exception.
- Knowing failure to provide covered services or necessary care to the members of an HMO.
- Patient dumping. The anti-dumping statute (known as the Emergency Medical Treatment and Active Labor Act of 1986 [EMTALA]) requires that all emergency rooms participating in Medicare provide the proper medical screening examination to determine whether a patient has an emergency medical condition. If the patient has such a condition, the hospital must either stabilize him or her or appropriately transfer the patient to a more suitable hospital.

Voluntary Disclosure

The OIG encourages providers to report suspected fraud or abuse by considering a voluntary disclosure. Because the government cannot monitor all Medicare and federal healthcare programs at once, the responsibility for self-monitoring falls on healthcare providers and their compliance program officers and committee. Physicians, providers, and other employees should be able and willing to govern themselves, correct problems as they see them, make repayments as necessary, and work with the government and the OIG to resolve any outstanding issues.

The OIG's voluntary self-disclosure program has four prerequisites:

1. The disclosure must be on behalf of an entity rather than an individual
2. The disclosure must be truly voluntary (i.e., no pending proceeding or investigation)
3. The entity must disclose the nature of the wrongdoing as well as the extent of the harm it may have already caused to Medicare or other federal programs
4. The entity must not be the subject of a bankruptcy proceeding before or after the self-disclosure

Requirements for all disclosures

The following items should be included as part of all disclosures:

- Contact information, type of healthcare provider, provider identification number(s), and tax identification numbers
- If owned or controlled by a system or network, an organizational chart with the contact information for all related entities
- Contact information of the designated representative for the disclosure
- Concise statement of all relevant details related to the disclosure
- A statement of the criminal, civil, or administrative laws that may have been violated
- The federal healthcare programs affected
- An estimation of damages
- A description of the corrective actions taken upon discovery
- A statement about whether the matter is currently under inquiry by a government agency or contractor
- The name of the individual authorized to enter into a settlement
- A certification by the disclosing party or entity

Compliance officers should be mindful of the fact that additional requirements may apply depending on the nature of the disclosure. For example, there are various requirements for false billing and additional requirements for disclosures involving excluded persons. Finally, additional requirements exist for disclosures related to the Anti-Kickback Statute and the Stark Law. The self-disclosure process is not available for potential violations solely related to the Stark Law. Entities and organizations must implicate either the Anti-Kickback Statute or both the Anti-Kickback Statute and the Stark Law.

If the voluntary disclosure relates to an inadvertent billing issue, the provider may be able to reprocess the claims to repay any amounts identified as overpayments and rebill such claims using the correct payment codes or work directly with the fiscal intermediary or carrier regarding the repayment.

The OIG's self-disclosure protocol should be used if a provider discovers intentional billing issues or fraud and abuse activities.

What Policies and Procedures Should Include

An entity's written policies and procedures should prove that it has a strong compliance program in place, as well as a willingness to comply with current regulations. Communication is key—policies should allow effective understanding of complex issues for a variable audience. As a compliance officer, you help develop and implement policies that need to take into account the wide variety of employees and departments, from clinical staff to administrative staff departments such as finance, that must understand and follow them.

According to guidance set forth by the OIG specific to billing, policies and procedures developed by organizations should do the following:

- Ensure accurate and timely documentation of all services prior to billing.
- Emphasize that claims should be submitted with appropriate documentation that is maintained and available for audit and review. Such documentation may include patient records and should record the time spent performing the service that led to the entry, as well as the identity of the person providing the service. The hospital and its medical staff may wish to establish other documentation guidelines as appropriate.
- Ensure that practitioner and hospital records and medical notes used as a basis for claim submissions are organized properly and legibly so they can be audited and reviewed.
- Insist that diagnoses and procedures reported on reimbursement claims be based on medical records and other documentation. The documentation necessary for accurate code assignment should be made available to coding staff members.
- Indicate that compensation for billing department coders and billing consultants should not provide any financial incentive to upcode claims.

Outpatient Services

The OIG continues to focus its attention on outpatient services rendered in connection with an inpatient stay. It advises hospitals to adopt the following measures:

- Use computer software to identify any outpatient services that may not be billed separately from an inpatient stay
- Implement a periodic manual review to determine the appropriateness of billing each outpatient service claim (this should be conducted by one or more appropriately trained employees who are familiar with such billing rules)
- Examine any potential bills for outpatient services rendered to a patient at the hospital, within the applicable time period

In addition to the guidelines described above, the hospital may choose to do the following for postsubmission testing:

- Adopt and maintain a periodic postsubmission random testing process that examines or reexamines previously submitted claims for accuracy
- Inform the fiscal intermediary and any other appropriate government fiscal agents of the hospital's testing process
- Advise the appropriate government fiscal agents regarding any returns of overpayments for incorrectly submitted or paid claims
- Promptly reimburse the fiscal intermediary and the beneficiary for the amount of the claim paid by the government payer and any applicable deductibles or copayments if the claim has already been paid

Submission of Claims for Laboratory Services

A hospital should ensure that all claims for clinical and diagnostic laboratory testing services are accurate and that they correctly identify the services ordered by the physician (or other authorized requestor) and performed by the laboratory. The OIG recommends that a hospital's written policies and procedures state the following:

- The hospital bills for laboratory services only after they are performed
- The hospital bills only for medically necessary services
- The hospital bills only for those tests actually ordered by a physician and provided by the hospital laboratory
- The Current Procedural Terminology or Healthcare Common Procedural Coding System code used by the billing staff accurately describes the service that was ordered

- The coding staff submits only diagnostic information obtained from qualified personnel and contacts the appropriate personnel to obtain diagnostic information in the event that the individual ordering the test fails to provide such information
- The hospital documents receipt of diagnostic information obtained from a physician or the physician's staff after receiving the specimen and request for services
- Routine audits are conducted to assess the hospital's regulatory billing compliance

Physicians at Teaching Hospitals

Hospitals should ensure the following with respect to all claims submitted on behalf of teaching physicians:

- Only services that are actually provided and documented in accordance with the applicable regulations are billed
- The physician who provides or supervises the provision of services to a patient is responsible for the correct documentation of the rendered services
- The appropriate documentation is placed in the patient record and authenticated by the physician who provided or supervised the provision of services to the patient
- Physicians are responsible for ensuring that, in cases where evaluation and management (E/M) services are provided, the patient's medical record includes appropriate documentation of the applicable key components of the E/M service (e.g., patient history, physician examination, and medical decision-making) as well as documentation that adequately reflects the procedure performed
- Every physician documents his or her presence during the key portion of any service or procedure for which payment is sought

Cost Reports

Written policies should include procedures that ensure compliance with applicable statutes, regulations, program requirements, and private payer plans. The hospital's procedures should ensure that the following are true:

- Costs are not claimed unless they are based on appropriate and accurate documentation
- Allocations of costs to various cost centers are accurate and supportable by verifiable and auditable data
- Unallowable costs are not claimed for reimbursement
- Accounts containing allowable and unallowable costs are analyzed to determine the unallowable amount that should not be claimed for reimbursement

- Costs are classified properly
- Fiscal intermediary prior year audit adjustments are implemented and are either not claimed for reimbursement or claimed for reimbursement and clearly identified as protested amounts on the cost report
- All related parties are identified on Form 339, which is submitted with the cost report, and all related party charges are reduced to cost
- Requests for exceptions to the Tax Equity and Fiscal Responsibility Act of 1982 limits and the routine cost limits are properly documented and supported by verifiable and auditable data
- The hospital's procedures for reporting bad debts on the cost report are in accordance with federal statutes, regulations, guidelines, and policies
- Allocations from a hospital chain's home office cost statement to individual hospital cost reports are accurate and supportable by verifiable and auditable data
- Procedures are in place and documented for promptly notifying the Medicare fiscal intermediary (or any other applicable payer) and Medicaid of errors discovered after the hospital cost report's submission

Medical Necessity—Reasonable and Necessary Services

A compliance program should ensure that claims are submitted only for services that the entity has reason to believe are medically necessary and that were ordered by an appropriate healthcare professional.

Healthcare professionals must be well versed in the rules of medical necessity, as Medicare and other government and private healthcare plans will pay only for those services that meet appropriate medical necessity standards (in the case of Medicare, they must be "reasonable and necessary" services). In other words, providers cannot bill for services that do not meet the applicable standards. Staff members must be aware of this fact. A hospital should be able to provide documentation, such as patients' medical records and a healthcare professional's orders, to support the medical necessity of a service it provided.

The compliance officer should ensure that a clear, comprehensive document summarizing the medical necessity definitions, as well as the rules of the various government and private plans, is prepared and appropriately communicated to the staff.

Scope of Practice

Healthcare professionals providing professional services within hospitals have various skill sets. The compliance officer should ensure that there is a clear organizational understanding of scope of practice. For example, some state laws place limitations on the types of services that a medical assistant may provide. In some instances, a payer will not pay for services unless a physician is board certified. Above all, organizations need to be mindful that services being provided by healthcare professionals match the education and training they have received. The compliance officer should work with clinical leadership and other leaders to establish clear guidelines that are consistent with state and federal law.

Anti-Kickback and Self-Referral Concerns

Organizations should have policies and procedures in place to deal with federal and state anti-kickback statutes, as well as the Stark Law. Such policies should provide that the following are true:

- All of the organization's contracts and arrangements with referral sources comply with applicable statutes and regulations, including an applicable exception if the Stark Act is implicated
- The organization does not enter into financial arrangements that are designed to provide inappropriate remuneration to the organization in return for a physician providing services to federal healthcare program beneficiaries at that hospital
- Policies and procedures address and define the OIG's safe harbor regulations, which outline payment practices that would be immune to prosecution under the Anti-Kickback Statute

See Chapter 3 for more information on the Stark Law, including changes finalized in November 2020.

Bad Debts

A hospital should have a mechanism to review the following:

- Whether the hospital properly reports bad debts to Medicare
- All Medicare bad debt expenses claimed, to ensure that the hospital's procedures are in accordance with applicable federal and state statutes, regulations, guidelines, and policies
- Whether the hospital has appropriate and reasonable mechanisms in place regarding beneficiary deductible or copayment collection efforts and has not claimed as bad debts any routinely waived Medicare copayments and deductibles

If questions arise, the hospital may consult with the appropriate fiscal intermediary as to bad debt reporting requirements.

Credit Balances

An organization should create procedures that guarantee timely and accurate reporting of Medicare and other federal healthcare program credit balances. For example, it may redesignate segments of its information system to allow for the segregation of patient accounts reflecting credit balances. The organization could remove these accounts from active status and place them in a holding account pending the processing of a reimbursement claim to the appropriate program. An organization's information system should be able to print out individual patient accounts that reflect a credit balance in order to simplify tracking of credit balances.

An organization also should designate at least one person as responsible for the tracking, recording, and reporting of credit balances. As an additional safeguard, a comptroller or accountant should, on a monthly basis, review reports of credit balances and reimbursements or adjustments.

Retention of Records

The compliance program should provide guidance to the organization for the implementation of a records retention system. Such a system should establish policies and procedures regarding the creation, distribution, retention, storage, retrieval, and destruction of documents. The two types of documents developed under this system include the following:

- All records and documentation, including clinical and medical records and claims documentation, that are required by federal or state law for participation in healthcare programs
- All records necessary to protect the integrity of the organization's compliance process and to confirm the effectiveness of the program, including documentation that employees were adequately trained, reports from the organization's hotline (including the nature and results of any investigation conducted), modifications to the compliance program, self-disclosures, and the results of the organization's auditing and monitoring efforts

Understanding the OIG's Priorities

In its Strategic Plan, the OIG has outlined various areas of focus throughout future years. The Strategic Plan is broader than the previously mentioned *Work Plan;* however, compliance officers should understand its primary areas of focus in order to further educate the organization regarding risks or concerns.

The primary goal of the plan is to ensure the success of the OIG's mission is to fight fraud, waste, and abuse. In order to see success, the OIG has outlined three primary goals along with strategies. First, the OIG intends to use increasing amounts of data analysis and risk assessments to identify, investigate, and take action. This includes focusing on enforcement models such as the Medicare Fraud Strike Force. Second, the OIG has made it a primary goal to hold those parties accountable. Through partnerships with the DOJ and other healthcare fraud enforcement mechanisms, the program has been able to recover more than $7 for every $1 invested. Finally, the OIG intends to prevent and deter fraud, waste, and abuse. It aims to focus on promoting compliance and resolving noncompliance within organizations. Above all, the OIG intends to increase scrutiny and require effective compliance programs.

Compliance as an Element of a Performance Plan

When evaluating the performance of managers and supervisors, factor in adherence to the elements of the compliance program. Managers, along with other employees, should be periodically trained in new compliance policies and procedures. In addition, all managers and supervisors involved in coding, claims, and cost report development and submission processes should do the following:

- Discuss with all supervised employees the compliance policies and legal requirements applicable to their jobs
- Inform all supervised personnel that strict compliance with these policies and requirements is a condition of employment
- Disclose to all supervised personnel that the hospital will take disciplinary action, up to and including termination or revocation of privileges, for violation of these policies or requirements

Establishing a Compliance Officer and Committee

Designating the compliance officer

As previously discussed, the OIG recommends that every hospital and most organizations designate a compliance officer to carry out and enforce compliance activities. This responsibility may be the individual's sole duty or may be added to other management responsibilities, depending upon the size and resources of the organization and the complexity of the task. If the organization is large, the compliance officer should be a single role and, as a best practice, not a dual general counsel and compliance officer role. This helps ensure an optimal level of independence and objectivity.

The compliance officer is critical to the success of the program. Therefore, the officer should have sufficient funding and staffing to fully perform his or her responsibilities. The compliance officer should function as an independent and objective person who reviews and evaluates organizational compliance and privacy/confidentiality issues and concerns. The position should involve advising and recommending actions to be taken by the board of directors, management, and employees to ensure organizational compliance with the rules and regulations of regulatory agencies. The compliance officer's main duties include coordination and communication of the compliance plan, which involves planning, implementing, and monitoring the program.

Specifically, the compliance officer's primary responsibilities should include the following:

- Overseeing and monitoring the implementation of the compliance program
- Regularly reporting to the organization's governing body, CEO, and compliance committee on the progress of implementation; helping establish methods to improve the organization's efficiency and quality of services; and reducing the organization's vulnerability to fraud, abuse, and waste
- Periodically revising the program in light of legal and organizational changes, as well as changes in the policies and procedures of government and private payer health plans
- Developing, coordinating, and participating in a multifaceted educational and training program that focuses on the elements of the compliance program and that seeks to ensure that all appropriate employees and management know and comply with applicable federal and state standards
- Ensuring that independent contractors and agents who furnish medical services to the organization are aware of the requirements of the organization's compliance program with respect to coding, billing, and marketing
- Coordinating personnel issues with the organization's HR office
- Coordinating the organization's financial management in organizing internal compliance review and monitoring activities, including annual or periodic reviews of departments or specific risk areas
- Independently investigating and acting on matters related to compliance, including the flexible design and coordination of internal investigations (e.g., responding to reports of problems or suspected violations) and any resulting corrective action with all hospital departments, providers and subproviders, agents, and independent contractors if appropriate
- Developing policies and programs that encourage managers and employees to report suspected fraud and other improprieties without fear of retaliation
- Developing a process to screen all employees, physicians, independent contractors, and suppliers to ensure that they have not been debarred or excluded from participation in the federal or state healthcare programs

The compliance officer must have the authority to review all documents and other information relevant to compliance activities, including but not limited to patient records, billing record contracts, and records concerning the marketing efforts of the facility and the organization's arrangements with other parties (such as employees, professionals on staff, independent contractors, suppliers, agents, and hospital-based physicians). This policy enables the compliance officer to review contracts and obligations that may contain referral and payment issues in violation of the Anti-Kickback Statute, the physician self-referral prohibition, or other legal or regulatory requirements. During such review, the officer should seek the advice of legal counsel where appropriate.

Designating the committee

An organization's compliance committee should advise the compliance officer and assist in the implementation and monitoring of the compliance program. The committee's functions should include the following tasks:

- Become knowledgeable about the content and operation of the organization's compliance program
- Review any actions taken to ensure that they are consistent with standards and expectations
- Discuss necessary disciplinary actions to be taken against those who have violated hospital policy
- Review audit results and make recommendations as appropriate
- Approve annual compliance program work plans
- Approve hiring of outside consultants
- Ensure that the compliance officer has the necessary resources to effectively perform his or her role
- Facilitate reporting of compliance activities to the board

The committee may also serve other functions as an organization gradually adopts a culture of compliance. The compliance committee may be established as a separate operating committee from the board but maintain membership of board members and non-board members. As an organization's culture of compliance matures, it would be ideal for this committee to be composed of the compliance officer, a financial leader, a legal leader, an operational leader, and board members. This will ensure that the committee has a reasonable level of leadership and is able to act upon issues brought forth.

Developing Lines of Communication

Access to the compliance officer

Open lines of communication between the compliance officer and organization personnel are vital to a successful compliance program. These lines of communication should be robust, public, and easily accessible. To encourage communication and reporting of potential cases of fraud, develop and distribute written confidentiality and nonretaliation policies to all employees. The compliance committee also should develop several independent reporting paths for an employee to report fraud, waste, or abuse so that supervisors and other personnel cannot divert such reports. Employees should feel they can speak to or report information to the compliance officer confidentially and without fear of retaliation.

Disciplinary Guidelines

The OIG recommends that a compliance program includes guidance regarding disciplinary action for corporate officers, managers, employees, physicians, and other healthcare professionals who fail to comply with the organization's standards of conduct, its policies and procedures, or federal regulations.

For maximum effectiveness, a compliance program should include a written policy statement defining the levels of disciplinary action that may be imposed upon noncompliant individuals. Intentional or reckless noncompliance should subject transgressors to significant sanctions. Such sanctions could include warnings, suspension, privilege revocation (up to or including termination), or financial penalties. The standards of conduct should specify who is responsible for handling disciplinary problems. Department managers can handle some disciplinary actions, whereas others may have to be resolved by a senior hospital administrator.

Employees should be made aware that disciplinary action will be taken fairly and equitably, whether the transgressor is a new hire or the organization's CEO. Equitable treatment is critical to an organization's culture of compliance.

Screening new employees

The OIG recommends that organizations carefully screen all new employees. This could include a thorough background investigation and a reference check. Employment applications should specifically require applicants to disclose any criminal convictions or exclusion actions. In addition, organization policies should prohibit the hiring of any individual who is listed as debarred, excluded, or otherwise ineligible for participation in federal healthcare programs.

Developing corrective action initiatives

Uncorrected misconduct can seriously endanger the mission, reputation, and legal status of an organization. It is therefore very important that the chief compliance officer or other management official promptly investigate suspected noncompliance and take steps to correct the problem. Such steps may include an immediate referral to criminal/civil law enforcement authorities, a corrective action plan, a report to the government, and/or the submission of any overpayments.

Reporting noncompliance

If the compliance officer or committee discovers evidence of misconduct or noncompliance and has reason to believe that the misconduct may violate criminal, civil, or administrative law, the discoverer should report the existence of misconduct to the appropriate governmental authority within a reasonable time period. It is recommended that such reports be made within 60 days after determining that a violation occurred and that they include the amount of any overpayment.

Prompt reporting is important because it demonstrates the organization's good faith and willingness to work with governmental authorities to correct and remedy compliance problems. More importantly, if the reporting provider becomes the target of an investigation, reporting such conduct will be considered a mitigating factor by the OIG and DOJ in determining administrative sanctions such as penalties, assessments, and exclusion.

Chapter 3
Key Regulations for Compliance

This chapter will discuss the regulations, guidelines, and statutes to which healthcare facilities must adhere. Healthcare is one of the most highly regulated industries in the world. Adherence to these laws is critical; therefore, a compliance officer must understand the complexity within these statutes and regulations.

Legal Counsel and Education

All compliance officers should ensure that they have immediate access to an attorney who specializes in healthcare regulatory compliance. This individual can work within the organization or may be in private practice. Such access to legal counsel is critical to the compliance officer being able to provide independent and objective insight into an organization's compliance with certain laws and regulations. In addition, a compliance officer should receive regular education on key regulations. Doing so will ensure that the individual is in a position to best educate the organization on changes to regulations and statutes.

U.S. Sentencing Guideline Overview

Congress created the sentencing guidelines in 1987 to meet several goals: to create uniform sentencing for different regions of the country, to stiffen penalties for drug-related and violent offenses, and to guarantee tougher sentences for white-collar criminals. The guidelines created a matrix of sentencing ranges depending on each defendant's criminal history and crime. To deviate from these ranges, judges had to find very unusual circumstances.

In 1991, Congress introduced guidelines for sentencing organizations, as opposed to sentencing individuals. These rules established mandatory fines rather than sentences (given that an organization cannot be sentenced to prison) and set a scale based on the organization's size, the nature of the crime, how the organization discovered the crime, and how the organization handled the problem. These new regulations planted the first seeds of compliance and compliance programs in the sentencing guidelines.

Then, in April 2004, the U.S. Sentencing Commission announced proposed revisions to the federal organizational sentencing guidelines to toughen the criteria for effective compliance and ethics programs. These changes made the standards for such programs more rigorous and put greater responsibility on boards of directors and executives to oversee and manage compliance programs. The guidelines also incorporated the concept of testing a compliance program for effectiveness.

The sentencing guidelines state the following:

- An organization's leadership and governing authority must be knowledgeable about the content and operation of its compliance program
- An organization's governing authority must exercise reasonable oversight of the program's implementation and effectiveness, including resource allocation
- Designated high-level personnel should be assigned direct responsibility for ensuring the program's implementation and effectiveness
- Personnel responsible for the compliance program should be given sufficient resources and should report directly to the governing authority
- An organization should create effective training programs for the governing authority, leadership, employees, and agents, as appropriate
- An organization should audit and monitor its programs for effectiveness and should conduct ongoing risk assessments to refine the program and reduce the risk of violations
- An organization should have a form of anonymous reporting, such as a hotline
- An organization should adopt appropriate incentives and disciplinary measures to ensure reporting of violations, compliance, and correction of violations

Although the guidelines are not mandatory, they are still important, as they advise organizations on how to implement and monitor compliance with laws and regulations. For example, the guidelines state that "compliance and ethics programs shall be reasonably designed, implemented, and enforced so that the program is generally effective in preventing and detecting criminal conduct" (USSC, 2013).

The amended guidelines zero in on boards of directors and executives, requiring them to oversee and manage their organizations' compliance and ethics programs. Because of these guidelines, directors and executives should take an active role in the structure and operation of compliance initiatives.

Guide to the guidelines

Federal trial judges use the guidelines, which apply to for-profit and nonprofit organizations, to determine sentences (e.g., fines, restitution, and probation conditions) for corporations convicted of federal crimes, including healthcare fraud.

The Office of Inspector General (OIG) also relies on this framework. It has traditionally incorporated organizational sentencing guidelines into its official compliance guidance for various sectors of the healthcare industry.

Although the OIG proclamations are framed as guidance to the industry—not as mandatory regulations—they become part of the yardstick against which, with hindsight, the OIG measures alleged corporate misconduct and determines whether administrative, civil, or even criminal penalties are appropriate.

The best way to avoid running into trouble for compliance violations is to show that your organization has an effective compliance program. If a problem is detected, you can leverage the problem through a strong and effective compliance program, especially if the problem was discovered as a result of your compliance initiatives. An effective program will demonstrate that you have implemented policies and procedures, that they are effective, and that your organization will do everything it can to comply with laws and regulations.

Recovery Audit Contractor Permanent Program

The Tax Relief and Healthcare Act of 2006 made the Recovery Audit Contractor (RAC) program permanent and expanded the RAC program to all 50 states as of 2010. The Centers for Medicare & Medicaid Services (CMS) has stated that the "goal of the recovery audit program is to identify improper payments made on claims of healthcare services provided to Medicare beneficiaries. Improper payments may be overpayments or underpayments." The contractors are paid on a contingency fee basis on the overpayments and underpayments they find as a result of a review of a provider. The RAC program began as a demonstration project to identify improper payments. During the three-year demonstration, RACs identified more than $1 billion in payments that were recognized as improper.

CMS has designated four RAC providers; each is responsible for approximately one-quarter of the country. The primary responsibilities of the RAC providers include identifying improper payments through chart reviews and software programs. Chart reviews are known as complex reviews; these types of reviews often occur if further review is needed when a claim may clearly contain errors. Software reviews, or automated reviews, highlight payments that are clearly deemed improper. Through these two methods, RACs are able to identify improper payments in different ways.

Providers should have a process for responding to a RAC request. Compliance officers should designate certain individuals or departments to receive and respond to the request. Providers should review all records responsive to an RAC request to ensure that the records to be delivered to the RAC are accurate and complete and to determine whether there are any issues in the responsive documentation prior to delivery. CMS has encouraged healthcare providers to conduct internal assessments to ensure that submitted claims comply with the Medicare rules.

Other steps that healthcare providers may consider taking include the following:

- Identifying trends of improper payments by reviewing the RACs' websites and pinpointing any patterns of denied claims within their own practice or facility
- Implementing procedures to promptly respond to RAC requests for medical records
- Filing an appeal before the 120-day deadline if a provider disagrees with an RAC determination
- Keeping track of denied claims and correcting previous errors
- Determining what corrective actions need to be taken to ensure compliance with Medicare's requirements and to avoid submitting incorrect claims in the future

False Claims Act Defined

The federal False Claims Act (FCA) imposes civil and, in some cases, criminal liability on organizations (and individuals) that knowingly make or cause to be made false or fraudulent claims to the government.

Such claims can be false or fraudulent due to intention or due to reckless disregard for their accuracy. An FCA violation can result in penalties of up to $11,000 per false claim, plus three times the amount of the damages that the government sustains. In addition, the government can exclude violators from Medicare, Medicaid, and other government healthcare programs. Because of the reckless disregard element, providers should audit and monitor the accuracy of the claims they submit. If unintentional errors are detected, corrective action must be implemented.

In 2009, the Fraud Enforcement Recovery Act (FERA) amended the FCA to impose liability when an individual avoids or decreases an obligation. Obligations are broadly defined but include a duty to refrain from retaining overpayments. Therefore, because of FERA, knowingly retaining overpayments can become an FCA violation if the obligation is not reported and refunded within a specific time frame once identified. Compliance officers should be mindful of the broad definition of "knowingly" under the FCA.

In addition to increased liability regarding overpayments, compliance officers should also recognize the employee aspect of the FCA. Often, employees of an organization may notice issues concerning billing and bring an action under the FCA. Compliance officers should maintain an open dialogue with these employees as the employees may seek to bring a *qui tam* lawsuit, in which a private individual brings a suit on the government's behalf.

Finally, with respect to employee protection, FERA implemented retaliatory action provisions. Above all, FERA has increased liability under the FCA and ensured transparency among organizations, preventing them from retaliating against employees with such concerns.

Each year fines and settlements under the FCA result in billions being paid back to the federal government. Although the FCA is not strictly limited to healthcare organizations, most FCA fines and settlements involve healthcare organizations.

Medicaid Fraud Enforcement

Medicaid fraud enforcement is one of the top enforcement priorities of the government. Through the Deficit Reduction Act (DRA), Congress provided significant financial resources targeted at Medicaid fraud and abuse. The DRA required the implementation of the Medicare Integrity Program at CMS, increased funding for Medicaid fraud through the OIG, gave states incentives to enact false claims laws similar to the FCA, and required employee training on the FCA and its whistleblower provisions.

Similar to Medicare fraud and abuse initiatives, states are now conducting aggressive Medicaid fraud and abuse reviews. Because of the federal mandate to implement state-specific false claims acts, Medicaid fraud units will have powers similar to Medicare fraud and abuse investigations under the FCA. States have established Medicaid Fraud Control Units (MFCU) that provide oversight regarding Medicaid fraud investigations. Each MFCU operates under the administrative oversight of the OIG and must be recertified annually.

The financial value of recoveries for states can be high. For example, in 2017, states recovered nearly $2 billion from the MCFUs. This resulted in a return on investment of $6.52 for every dollar spent on investigations.

In addition to the MFCUs, states are now required to contract with RACs to identify payment issues for Medicaid services. Because of the increased focus on Medicaid fraud and abuse, providers should be reviewing their Medicaid claims to ensure compliance with billing requirements.

Overview of Sarbanes-Oxley

The Sarbanes-Oxley Act (SOX) gives audit committees and independent directors responsibilities for corporate governance and oversight. Although SOX applies only to publicly traded companies, the following provisions should be adopted by privately owned and nonprofit healthcare organizations:

- 201 and 202—Nonaudit services and advance approval. These provisions highlight the increased sensitivity the board must demonstrate when determining which nonaudit services an outside auditor can perform.
- 301—Increased role of audit committees, including enhanced relationships with the auditor and the audit process. This provision potentially holds the boards and senior management more accountable for the process and the quality of audits.
- 302—Certification of reports. This provision increases senior management's responsibility for internal controls and the content of the financial report.
- 303—Improper influence on conduct of audit. This rule prohibits officers and directors from fraudulently influencing or misleading an independent auditor as he or she reviews the organization's financial records.
- 406—Code of ethics. This provision requires implementation of a code of ethics for senior financial officers.
- 407—Financial expert on audit committee. Although private companies are not required to have a financial expert on the audit committee, this provision places greater focus on the composition of the board and the audit committee. Each should be familiar enough with financial and accounting matters to be able to scrutinize and supervise the financial reporting process.
- 802—Document destruction or altercation. SOX enacts substantial criminal penalties for destroying or altering records or documents in order to impede a government investigation. It also adopts rules concerning the retention of documents created, sent, or received in connection with an audit.

SOX is the most comprehensive federal securities law affecting public companies since securities legislation was passed in 1933 and 1934, after the previous decade's stock market crash. SOX specifically regulates the activities of public companies—those companies whose securities are traded on an exchange such as the New York Stock Exchange (NYSE) or a quotation system such as the National Association of Securities Dealers Automated Quotations (NASDAQ) stock market index. However, many private and nonprofit organizations apply SOX principles as best practices in response to mounting external pressures from the legislative and regulatory sectors, as well as internal pressures from board members who sit on public company boards.

Compliance under SOX

Numerous requirements and restrictions have been created as a result of SOX and regulations promulgated under SOX. We will take a closer look at those that may be the most pertinent.

Code of ethics

A code of ethics or conduct refers to a standard established by a company to promote and encourage ethical conduct; full, accurate, timely, and understandable disclosures in public communications, in reports, and in documents filed with the Securities and Exchange Commission (SEC); and compliance with governmental laws, rules, and regulations. An effective code fosters timely internal reporting of code violations to an appropriate person, as well as accountability and adherence to ethics. A code should address conflicts of interest; corporate opportunities; confidentiality; fair dealing with customers, suppliers, competitors, and employees; protection and proper use of company assets; compliance with laws, rules, and regulations; reporting of any illegal or unethical behavior; and implementation of corrective action when problems or errors are detected. The code also should provide for an enforcement mechanism for compliance.

SOX requires companies to have a code of ethics that applies to senior management and officers responsible for the company's financial matters, such as auditing and public disclosures. NYSE and NASDAQ rules go one step further, requiring companies to have a code of conduct (not just ethics) that applies to all directors, officers, and employees. The rules also require that the code be publicly available, such as on a company's website. In addition, rules promulgated by the SEC under SOX require companies to disclose promptly (i.e., within four days) any waivers from the code's requirements that are granted to directors and executive officers. The code should govern the organization's operations and not be simply words on paper.

Responding to whistleblowers

A whistleblower is a company employee who provides information to a governmental entity or investigator regarding any conduct that the employee believes is a violation of laws, rules, or regulations. SOX mandates that companies provide whistleblower protections to employees who assist in proceedings relating to an alleged violation of securities laws or regulations. These protections prohibit officers, employees, contractors, subcontractors, and agents of the company from firing, demoting, or engaging in any other retaliation against a whistleblower.

To the extent that a whistleblower believes that he or she has suffered retaliation, the whistleblower may bring a federal private action against the company and its employees and agents to demand reinstatement and back pay. Whistleblower protection and the right of action create an environment in which employees can safely serve as watchdogs of the corporate practices of their companies, officers, and directors.

SOX also requires a company's audit committee to implement and promote procedures to receive, retain, and address employee complaints on internal accounting controls and audit matters. Such procedures include establishing a hotline for employees to provide uncensored reports of senior management's purported questionable acts. Reports from the hotline should be delivered through the audit committee to the board and management of the company so that issues may be addressed and corrective action implemented.

Internal controls

SOX requires management of public companies to assess and report on internal controls. Many companies have noted that this requirement is the most comprehensive and costly regulation under SOX.

In particular, public companies must design overarching internal controls over financial reporting, must report on such controls, and must require auditors to assess such controls. The importance of this requirement to pharmaceutical and life sciences companies involves internal controls over financial statements, billing practices, and other arrangements. Companies should ensure that such practices and arrangements are in compliance with the rules and regulations of Medicare, Medicaid, and other federal or state healthcare programs.

Employee training

To ensure compliance with SOX and to practice good corporate governance, companies should provide training on SOX and SOX-related requirements to all employees. This training should make management aware of its legal obligations and inform employees of these same obligations so that they may serve as whistleblowers should the need arise.

A good training program should explain how SOX requirements affect normal business practices. It should be live and interactive to ensure that all existing and new employees understand the need to comply with SOX, and it should be mandatory for all employees, with signatures documenting attendance. If documents are distributed, attendees should be required to certify that they have read and understood them. A good training program can foster compliance with the law and ethical behavior.

HIPAA Privacy Rule

The Health Insurance Portability and Accountability Act of 1996 (HIPAA) is a multifaceted piece of federal legislation that covers insurance portability, fraud enforcement, and administrative simplification.

Although HIPAA privacy and security issues are discussed in a later chapter, HIPAA is a fraud enforcement function that should not be overlooked. Administrative simplification includes the Privacy Rule and the Security Rule, which penalize individuals and organizations that fail to maintain the confidentiality of protected patient health information.

Components of HIPAA

The privacy regulation (i.e., final rule) says that physicians can discuss patient information with fellow providers. The regulations require physicians to make a reasonable effort to disclose and use only information that is necessary for treatment, securing payment, and conducting standard organizational duties, such as audits and data collection. In other words, physicians need to understand the ramifications of what they share, with whom, and where.

According to the regulation, privacy is an individual's right to control access and disclosure of his or her protected, individually identifiable health information. Security is an organization's responsibility to control the means by which this information remains confidential, such as controlling access to electronically stored information.

The proposed security standards under HIPAA support and further the intent of the privacy rule by complementing the privacy measures. Physicians have an important role in keeping their records and computer technology secure, particularly laptops and other portable devices containing patient notes.

Consequences of noncompliance

Failure to comply is not an option for physicians or other healthcare providers. The law, as written, provides a range of penalties for noncompliance. Context and intent govern the amount of the penalty. For physicians and other healthcare workers who knowingly release information inappropriately, the penalties can be stiff.

The penalties for breaking privacy rules go beyond fines and potential jail time—they could place a physician's license at risk. They also could lead to trials and damaging publicity for individuals and institutions.

Health Care Fraud Statute

The federal criminal Health Care Fraud Statute imposes liability on both public and private healthcare fraud. This statute prohibits a person from knowingly and willfully executing or attempting to execute a scheme to either defraud a healthcare benefit program or obtain property by false or fraudulent pretenses in connection with the delivery of or payment for healthcare services.

Any violation of this statute can result in a 10-year imprisonment term, restitution, and a fine.

Anti-Kickback Statute

The federal healthcare program Anti-Kickback Statute is a broad criminal statute that prohibits one person from "knowingly and willfully" giving (or offering to give) "remuneration" to another if the payment is intended to "induce" the recipient to "refer" an individual to a person for the furnishing of any item or service for which payment may be made, in whole or in part, under a federal healthcare program (i.e., a "covered item or service"); "purchase," "order," or "lease" any covered item or service; "arrange for" the purchase, order, or lease of any covered item or service; or "recommend" the purchase, order, or lease of any covered item or service. The Anti-Kickback Statute also prohibits the solicitation or receipt of remuneration for any of these purposes.

"Remuneration" includes anything of value. The term "inducement" has been interpreted to cover any act intended to influence a person's reason or judgment. Some courts have held that as long as one purpose of the payment at issue is to induce referrals, the Anti-Kickback Statute is implicated. Under this "one-purpose" rule, an arrangement may implicate the Anti-Kickback Statute even if inducing referrals is not the primary purpose of the payment and even where there are other, legitimate reasons for the arrangement. However, courts also have recognized that a party may hope or expect that a particular arrangement will result in referrals without necessarily triggering the one-purpose rule.

Because the Anti-Kickback Statute is so broad, it covers various common and nonabusive arrangements. Recognizing the breadth of this statute, Congress and the OIG have established numerous statutory and regulatory safe harbors. An arrangement that fits squarely into a safe harbor is immune from prosecution under the Anti-Kickback Statute.

The safe harbors tend to be very narrow, and the OIG takes the position that immunity is afforded only to those arrangements that "precisely meet" all of the conditions of a safe harbor—that is, material or substantial compliance is insufficient. Moreover, safe harbors do not exist for every type of arrangement that does (or may) implicate the Anti-Kickback Statute. Common safe harbors protect arrangements such as employment, leasing of space and equipment, purchased services, and discounts. If all elements of a safe harbor are not met, the arrangement will not violate the Anti-Kickback Statute unless it can be proven that the parties intended to induce referrals or purchases through the arrangement.

Another concern regarding the Anti-Kickback Statute is whether a violation of the statute constitutes a violation of other healthcare fraud and abuse laws. The Stark Law is discussed below; however, healthcare reform specifically amended the Anti-Kickback Statute to include that a violation of the statute constitutes a false or fraudulent claim for purposes of the FCA. Above all, compliance officers should understand that an individual does not need to have actual knowledge of the Anti-Kickback Statute, nor does the individual need specific intent to commit a violation. Therefore, the Anti-Kickback Statute should be a primary area in which compliance officers educate others in their organizations.

In November 2020, the federal government finalized changes that revise and clarify various regulatory exceptions and safe harbors and impacts both the Anti-Kickback Statute and the Stark Law. The provisions of the final rule are effective January 19, 2021. The following is a summary of the key changes that affect the Anti-Kickback Statute:

- **Value-based arrangements.** The OIG, similar to the exceptions created by CMS, created safe harbors under the Anti-Kickback Statute for value-based arrangements. The safe harbors under the Anti-Kickback Statute consistently track the value-based arrangements exceptions discussed later in this chapter with the corresponding Stark Law exceptions, although in some cases the percentages are different. By way of example, under the safe harbor, a "substantial downside financial risk" is 30% instead of 10% under the Stark Law exception.
- **Patient engagement and support safe harbor.** The OIG, through the final rules, added a new safe harbor permitting a DHS entity to provide patient health support resources in order to improve the beneficiaries' health quality, outcomes, and efficiency. The value of these support items is capped at $500 per beneficiary per year. The safe harbor, however, only applies to entities that qualify as a "value-based enterprise."
- **CMS-sponsored model arrangements and CMS-sponsored model patient incentives.** The OIG has added safe harbors permitting an entity to provide patient incentives focused on quality and health outcomes for beneficiaries covered under either the CMS Innovation Center or the Medicare Shared Savings Program. These safe harbors only apply if a beneficiary is covered by a CMS-sponsored program and any incentive provided to a beneficiary must further a goal of the CMS-sponsored program and have a connection with the beneficiaries' healthcare.
- **Cybersecurity technology and related services.** The OIG adopted a new safe harbor similar to the Stark Law exception, discussed later in this chapter, related to the donation of cybersecurity technology and related services.
- **Local transportation safe harbor.** The OIG, in the final rules, modified the mile distance in the local transportation safe harbor. First, for residents of rural areas, the OIG extended the mileage distance from 50 to 75 miles. Second, for transportation of a beneficiary upon discharge the 25-mile limit on transportation to the patient's residence has been eliminated. However, to fit within this safe harbor, the transportation must still be "local." The elimination of the 25-mile limit provides greater flexibility for entities that have a service area greater than a 25-mile radius. The compliance officer must still ensure that the transportation is deemed to be "local" and the transportation must be for transporting the beneficiary from the facility to the beneficiary's residence or post-discharge facility.

- **Personal services and management contracts safe harbor.** Prior to the final rules, the "aggregate" compensation in an independent contractor arrangement was required to be set in advance. By contrast, the personal service arrangements exception under the Stark Law only required that the methodology used to calculate the compensation must be set in advance. The OIG, in the final rules, modified the personal services and management contracts safe harbor to more align with the personal service arrangements exception under the Stark Law. Now, the safe harbor only requires that the methodology of the compensation be set in advance and no longer requires that the aggregate compensation be set in advance. Further, the OIG eliminated the requirement that the exact schedule, precise length, and exact charge for each interval of a part-time arrangement be set in advance. This modification to the personal services and management contracts safe harbor will permit many independent contractor arrangements to comply with the safe harbor that previously would not have complied with the safe harbor due to the strict requirement regarding the aggregate compensation being set in advance.
- **Electronic health records items and services.** Prior to the final rules, the electronic health records safe harbor, and corresponding Stark Law exception, required that the 15% cost sharing be paid in advance. The safe harbor, and the Stark Law exception, have now been revised to permit the recipient of such items and services to pay the 15% cost sharing at a "reasonable interval." This means, from a compliance perspective, recipients can pay the cost sharing amount after receipt but such payments will need to be monitored to ensure that such post-receipt payments are actually paid by the recipient.

Advisory opinions: Anti-Kickback Statute

The Anti-Kickback Statute, as discussed previously, is extremely broad and requires organizations to adhere to seemingly impossible requirements in order to have an arrangement within a safe harbor. However, because of the complexity of this statute and the overall breadth of arrangements that may be implicated, the OIG implemented a program in which organizations may submit proposals for the purpose of seeing whether such an arrangement meets a safe harbor. These advisory opinions, when published, provide a detailed analysis regarding real arrangements that may or may not violate the Anti-Kickback Statute. Compliance officers should regularly consider these advisory opinions and actively educate others in their organizations with any updates or new opinions.

Stark Law

The federal physician self-referral law, commonly referred to as the "Stark Law," establishes two basic prohibitions:

1. First, a physician who has a financial relationship with an entity may not refer a Medicare beneficiary to that entity for the furnishing of services known as designated health services (DHS). This is referred to as the referral prohibition.

2. Second, a provider may not bill for improperly referred services. This is referred to as the billing prohibition.

Both of these prohibitions apply unless an applicable exception has been met. If an exception has not been met, then the entity that collects payment must refund all collected amounts received through the improper referrals, and civil monetary penalties may be enforced up to $15,000 per violation.

The primary motivation behind the Stark Law, according to CMS, is preventing the overutilization of services. For example, prior to the Stark Law, a physician could send labs to be analyzed at a laboratory owned by the physician. This created two problematic issues. First, the physician may be motivated to increase profits for the laboratory he or she owns. Second, this incentive to profit leads to overutilization of healthcare services.

The Stark Law has developed over the years; from its initial goal of preventing overutilization, it now impacts any relationship a physician has with a DHS entity, including hospitals. Generally, a profit motive also hinders the focus on quality, which is why the Stark Law has expanded into many different areas. It is therefore important for compliance officers to understand how to analyze whether the Stark Law is implicated.

In November 2020, the federal government finalized changes that revise and clarify various regulatory exceptions and safe harbors and impacts both the Anti-Kickback Statute and the Stark Law. The provisions of the final rule are effective January 19, 2021. From a compliance perspective, these modifications provide new opportunities for quality and efficiency and greater flexibility in the establishment of financial arrangements with referring physicians. Although, in some cases, greater flexibility is allowed by the OIG and CMS, the monitoring burden has not decreased. The compliance officer must ensure that he or she is aware of changes and is responsible for providing education and training on these changes.

How to analyze whether the Stark Law applies

The first question is whether a physician is making a referral. A referral is a request by a physician for an item, service, or plan of care. Regulations have further broadened this definition; a referral can now include any order, request, or type of plan for a patient.

If a referral has been made, the second question is whether the referral is for DHS. Common DHSs include hospital inpatient and outpatient services, laboratory tests, radiology diagnostic tests, physical therapy, and home health services.

The third question is whether the physician (or an immediate family member of the physician) has a financial relationship with the entity furnishing the DHS. This is an important question, as there are four different types of financial relationships:

1. Direct ownership: The physician owns or has an interest in the entity.

2. Indirect ownership: The physician owns or has an interest in an entity that owns or has an interest in the entity furnishing the DHS.
3. Direct compensation: The physician receives remuneration directly from an entity furnishing DHS.
4. Indirect compensation: An example may suffice for this final section category. Assume that a physician owns a telephone company and that the telephone company provides services to the hospital. This may implicate an indirect compensation arrangement because the hospital could induce referrals through increased payments to the phone company. If a financial relationship does exist, the Stark Law is implicated and needs to qualify for an exception.

The final question is whether an exception exists.

Stark Law exceptions

Stark Law exceptions are highly complex and technical. However, if the Stark Law applies to an arrangement, a Stark Law exception must be met lest the arrangement potentially violate the law.

There are various exceptions, including general exceptions, the *investment and ownership* exceptions, *direct compensation* exceptions, and an *indirect compensation* exception. For example, the general exceptions may apply to all four categories of arrangements. One of the most common methods for ensuring that an arrangement meets a Stark Law exception is to ensure that fair market value (FMV) compensation is paid between the DHS entity and the referring physician. FMV is included as a component of meeting many such exceptions, including common exceptions, such as the employment exception or the complex exception for indirect compensation arrangements. FMV, in addition to other important exceptions, is discussed below.

Fair market value

Generally, FMV as defined by the Stark Law (see Figure 3.1) is assessed for services provided by a physician, assets, and any type of rental payments for office space or equipment. Organizations can seek to establish FMV through the use of outside consultants who can properly assess both the legal and financial considerations. Although certain exceptions provide an FMV assessment based purely on the value of space or equipment, most focus on the facts and circumstances applied to the value of a service, such as call coverage. As a best practice, organizations should ensure that an FMV assessment is part of an overall legal defensibility analysis performed by an attorney. Too often, organizations forget that this requirement, although having a foundation in finance, is a legal requirement.

FIGURE 3.1
Stark Law Definition of FMV
The value in arm's length transactions, consistent with the general market value, and, with respect to rentals or leases, the value of rental property for general commercial purposes (not taking into account its intended use) and, in the case of a lease of space, not adjusted to reflect the additional value the prospective lessee or lessor would attribute to the proximity or convenience to the lessor where the lessor is a potential source of patient referrals to the lessee.
42 USC §1395nn(h)(3)

Although establishing FMV is integral to many Stark Law exceptions, compliance officers should be aware that, with respect to physician compensation, such an analysis is a legal question. For example, CMS has stated that reliance on an outside appraiser for the FMV opinion is relevant with respect to the intent of the party; however, ultimately it must be accurate and must comply with an exception. Therefore, compliance officers should ensure that opinions contain sufficient analysis to defend their arrangements in a court of law. Above all, establishing FMV is considered a legal question and should be defensible.

Nonmonetary compensation exception

One of the most important exceptions for compliance officers is the nonmonetary compensation exception. The primary reasons this exception is important is that it is often overlooked within organizations, it is tough to track, and there is a high risk of violation when multiple physicians are involved. The exception allows an organization to provide compensation to a physician, not including cash or cash equivalents, so long as such benefit does not exceed the annual designated amount provided by CMS, which was $423 at the time of publication but which increases annually (see *www.cms.gov/Medicare/Fraud-and-Abuse/PhysicianSelfReferral/CPI-U_Updates*). For example, a gift basket to a physician may not violate the Stark Law so long as it meets this exception.

In addition to the aggregate amount limit, there are three conditions:

1. The benefit cannot be determined based upon the volume or the value of referrals
2. The benefit is not solicited by the physician or groups
3. The maximum benefit cannot be aggregated to make a larger gift to a group

In the event that a hospital does exceed the limit, it may still be deemed to be in compliance if the value of the excess is no more than 50% of the limit and the excess is returned by the end of the calendar year or within 180 days, whichever is earlier. In addition, if a benefit, item, or service is used on the hospital's campus and provided to all members in the same specialty and is provided only during periods when the medical staff is providing services at the hospital, and if the benefit is less than $36 (increases annually; see *www.cms.gov/Medicare/Fraud-and-Abuse/PhysicianSelfReferral/CPI-U_Updates.html*), then such benefits would be considered compensation meeting the medical staff incidental benefits exception.

This exception creates considerable operational issues for compliance officers. Many hospital staff members regularly meet with physicians and may provide benefits that are not tracked. Compliance officers should ensure that the hospital staff is educated with respect to this exception and make sure that there is a method for tracking such spending.

Above all, compliance officers should make it clear that any nonmonetary benefits provided to physicians must be reviewed by the compliance officer prior to any such benefit being provided.

Value-based arrangements

As part of the November 2020 changes to the Stark Law, through the final rules, CMS established three new, permanent exceptions for value-based arrangements and definitions for terminology integral to such a system. The new value-based arrangements are codified at 42 *CFR* §411.357(aa)(1)-(3) and generally referred to as follows:

- Value-based arrangements with full financial risk
- Value-based arrangements with meaningful downside financial risk
- Value-based arrangements provided that the stipulated requirements under such arrangements are met

The value-based arrangements are driven by precise definitions, including specific regulatory definitions. Before entering into any value-based arrangement, careful consideration should be applied to each definition to ensure that the arrangement conforms to the specific definitions in the exception.

Full financial risk

This exception permits a value-based enterprise to assume full financial risk for all patient care services covered by a payer for a targeted patient population. Full financial risk for the costs of such patient care services must be assumed within 12 months after the commencement of the value based arrangement. The savings can be divided amongst all participants.

Meaningful downside financial risk

This exception applies when the value-based enterprise participants assume meaningful downside financial risk for the patient care services covered by a payer. The final rules define "meaningful downside financial risk" to be at least 10% of the remuneration received by the value-based enterprise/physicians. Under this arrangement, the enterprise/physician is responsible for the cost of all specified patient-care items for each patient in the applicable target patient population. The savings can be divided amongst all participants.

General value-based arrangements

The general value-based arrangement exception permits the value-based enterprise/physicians to establish any value-based arrangement as long as "outcome measures" are met. Under this exception, as long as there is an enhancement in quality, reduction in costs to the payer, or growth in expenditures, in-kind items or services can be provided to the value-based enterprise/physicians. In the final rule, CMS emphasized that simply "maintaining quality," although important, would not qualify for the exception, as it applies to the enhancement or improvement of quality as opposed to the maintenance of quality. The financial arrangement between the value-based enterprise and its participants is limited on to non-monetary/in-kind items or services that further the value-based mission.

Other recent changes to the Stark Law

The following is a summary of other key changes to the Stark Law finalized by the federal government in November 2020.

Limited remuneration to a physician.

The final rule created a new exception whereby a DHS entity can provide limited compensation to a physician up to $5,000 per year. Unlike the non-monetary compensation exception, discussed later in this chapter, this exception permits financial compensation to be paid to a physician on a limited basis. For example, if a DHS entity needed to hire a medical director or compensate a physician for call coverage services on a limited basis, as long as the annual compensation paid by the DHS entity to the physician does not exceed $5,000 during a calendar year, such compensation paid would be compliant with a Stark Law exception even without the arrangement being in writing and signed by the parties. The compensation paid under this exception, however, will still need to meet the fair market value and commercial reasonableness requirements.

Isolated financial transactions

CMS modified this exception prohibiting it to be used for a single payment for multiple or repeated services. By way of example, the isolated financial transactions exception cannot be used to compensate a medical director for multiple days of service through a single payment.

Temporary non-compliance with writing and signature requirements

CMS provided significant leniency for "temporary non-compliance" with the signature and writing requirements. The final rule now permits the DHS entity and physicians to prepare the written arrangement and obtain signatures within 90 days of the commencement of the arrangement. Previously, the writing had to exist and the signatures could be delayed up to 90 days. Now CMS is permitting both the writing and the signatures to be obtained within 90 days of the commencement of the arrangement.

Commercial reasonableness

According to the final rules, an arrangement is "commercially reasonable" if "the particular arrangement furthers a legitimate business purpose of the parties to the arrangement and is sensible, considering the characteristics of the parties, including their size, type, scope, and specialty." This modification now focuses commercial reasonableness on the transaction between the parties instead of looking to the general market. CMS also stated in the final rules that "[a]n arrangement may be commercially reasonable even if it does not result in profit for one or more of the parties." Simply because a loss is generated on the physicians' direct services, such a loss does not, without other factors, mean that the arrangement is not commercially reasonable. In other words, an arrangement between a DHS entity and a referring physician can still be commercially reasonable even if the DHS entity generates a loss based upon the physicians' direct patient care services.

Taking into account volume or value of referrals or other business generated standard

Many of the Stark Law exceptions prohibit compensation from taking into account the volume or value of referrals or other business generated between the parties. Prior to the November 2020 changes, this standard was not defined. The final rules clarify the standard by indicating that it applies based on whether the formula used to calculate compensation varies based on the physicians' referrals or other business generated that correlates with the number or value of referrals or business generated.

Indirect compensation arrangement definition

Historically, in order to meet the indirect compensation arrangement definition, the closest compensation arrangement to the referring physician needed to be analyzed to determine whether the aggregate compensation varied with or took into account the volume or value of referrals. Under the final rules, an indirect compensation arrangement must be one of the following:

- The individual unit of compensation (i.e., compensation per wRVU) must not be defensible from a fair market value perspective
- The aggregate compensation received by the referring physician includes compensation based on the referring physician's referrals or other business generated for the DHS entity as a variable
- To meet this component of the indirect compensation arrangement definition, the referring physician's compensation must change or correlate with the number or value of referrals or other business generated by the referring physician for the DHS entity.

Designated health services—inpatient

CMS clarified the designated health services definition as it relates to hospital inpatients. If a physician orders a test or performs a consultation and the test or consultation does not impact the DRG billed, the referral or ordering of a test or service by a physician would not constitute a designated health service. This modification will be beneficial if a potential Stark Law issue arises with hospital-based specialties, such as interventional radiology or anesthesiology.

Period of disallowance

Previously, the Stark Law regulations generally defined the "period of disallowance" as the first referral to the DHS entity when the referring physician did not have a financial arrangement that conformed with a Stark Law exception and ended when the financial arrangement complied fully with a Stark Law exception. The final rule eliminated this "bright line" defined term. By eliminating this bright line test, CMS is providing greater flexibility to defining the period of disallowance.

Group practice definition

The final rules tweaked the group practice definition. The most significant modification in the final rules relates to "overall profits." Generally, it was believed the profits component of the group practice definition could be segregated based upon a service line (i.e., only cardiovascular surgeons in a multi-specialty practice). Now, CMS indicated that the "overall profits" component of the group practice definition means the "entire profits" of the group practice and cannot be based on components of segregated profits.

Rental of office space/equipment/time share leases

The rental of office space, equipment, and time share exceptions have required that the lessee be the "exclusive" user of the space or equipment. CMS clarified that multiple lessees (meaning multiple referring physicians/groups) can use the space and equipment as long as the lessor (usually a DHS entity) does not use it during the same time that lessee(s) are leasing the space and equipment. This is an important compliance clarification as managing part-time/time-shared use of space and equipment has been a compliance hot spot.

Cybersecurity technology and related services

Under a new exception, CMS permits DHS entities to donate cybersecurity technology and related services to referring physicians/groups. The donation of technology and services cannot take into account the volume or value of referrals or other business generated between the parties. The cybersecurity technology and related services must be "necessary and used predominantly to implement, maintain or re-establish effective cybersecurity," according to CMS.

Payments by a physician

The payments by a physician exception permits a referring physician to pay a DHS entity fair market value for items or services received that are not specifically excepted by another Stark Law exception. Previously, the payments by a physician exception specifically referenced the fair market value exception. The final rules deleted the reference to the fair market value exception. Therefore, as long as the payments by a referring physician to a DHS entity are not specifically excepted by another Stark Law exception, such as the rental of office space, the compensation paid by a referring physician to a DHS entity can comply with this exception for items or services received by the referring physician. The compensation paid by the referring physician must be at fair market value. Most notably, however, this exception does not require that the arrangement be in writing and signed by the parties or set in advance.

Employment exception and directed referrals

Under the employment exception, personal services exception, and others, CMS is now mandating compliance with requirements outlined in §411.354(d)(4). Historically, organizations could use section 411.354(d)(4) as a defensive mechanism to ensure that if their arrangement included processes that steered referrals, policies that directed referrals, or actual mandates of referrals, the process, policy, or mandate would not violate the volume or value standard. The 1998 update to the Stark Law included section 411.354(d)(4), which outlines this defensive mechanism to mitigate concern that this could violate the volume or value standard.

Under this defensive mechanism, it required that if an organization wished to avoid any risk under the volume or value standard, the arrangement would need to meet specific requirements under §411.354(d)(4).

If an organization fulfilled these requirements, under the previous CMS guidance, if processes, policies, or mandates on referrals existed, the arrangement would avoid liability under the volume or value standard.

FCA and the Stark Law

Compliance officers should be aware that an organization can incur both a Stark Law violation and an FCA violation for the same arrangement. This is important to note because the FCA allows triple damages and penalties up to $11,000 per claim. For any whistleblowers within organizations, reporting perceived violations can be extremely lucrative, as they may share the settlement with the government. Under the FCA, payments from the government must be false for a violation to have occurred. If there is a Stark Law violation in which reimbursement was sought and an exception has not been met, the claim for payment is considered false by the federal government.

For example, if a referring physician is renting equipment from a hospital and there is no written agreement, the arrangement would not meet the exception for rental of equipment under Stark. This arrangement would be in violation of the Stark Law, therefore making all referrals from the physician prohibited under federal law and false. By engaging in the prohibited relationship and submitting false claims to the federal government, this arrangement has now implicated the FCA.

Compliance officers must understand the risks of the Stark Law and how such arrangements may implicate other laws, including situations in which a Stark Law violation may constitute a false claim for the purpose of the FCA.

Anti-Kickback Statute vs. Stark Law

The Anti-Kickback Statute is similar in many respects to the Stark Law in terms of its overarching policy objectives and general prohibitions. By the same token, there are material differences between the two authorities, including the following:

- The Anti-Kickback Statute is a criminal statute, whereas the Stark Law provides for civil and administrative sanctions.
- The Anti-Kickback Statute has a "state of mind" (or scienter) requirement (i.e., in order to be convicted, a defendant must have acted "knowingly and willfully" to induce referrals or purchases). The Stark Law is a "strict liability" statute (i.e., the Stark Law's referral and billing prohibitions may be violated even if the physician, provider, or supplier did not intend to violate them).
- The Anti-Kickback Statute covers all federal healthcare programs (with the exception of the Federal Employee Health Benefits Program), whereas the Stark Law's referral and billing prohibitions currently apply only to Medicare. The Anti-Kickback Statute may be implicated by any type of arrangement involving any type of healthcare or nonhealthcare organization, whereas the Stark Law focuses on physicians (and their immediate family members) and their financial relationships with certain types of entities (e.g., hospitals) that perform or bill for DHS.

The Emergency Medical Treatment and Active Labor Act of 1986

The Emergency Medical Treatment and Active Labor Act of 1986 (EMTALA) is a federal statute that addresses how hospitals deliver emergency services to the public. In a nutshell, it requires emergency departments (ED) to provide a medical screening exam, conducted by a qualified medical staff professional, to patients who arrive on hospital property and who appear to need emergency medical services; this exam is performed to determine whether a patient has an emergency condition.

Congress enacted EMTALA following a series of well-publicized incidents in which hospital policy prevented patients in desperate need of emergency medical care from getting it because of their inability to pay. Known as the "anti-dumping" law, EMTALA prohibits hospital EDs from delaying care, refusing treatment, or transferring patients to another hospital based on inability to pay for services.

Because patients presenting to any area of the hospital may fall under EMTALA rules, all levels of hospital personnel must understand their obligations under the regulations. All staff working in the ED, labor and delivery, or psychiatric areas should be able to identify the extent and limits of their responsibilities and the legal risks attached to them.

Physicians and hospital staff who are unfamiliar with the EMTALA requirements are putting themselves at significant risk, as EMTALA enforcement is one of the government's top priorities.

SUPPORT for Patients and Communities Act

The Substance Use–Disorder Prevention that Promotes Opioid Recovery and Treatment (SUPPORT) for Patients and Communities Act is a law designed to focus on the opioid epidemic occurring in the United States. The law includes many provisions meant to curb illegal use of opioids and to create more safeguards when it comes to prescribing opioids. Compliance officers should ensure that their policies and procedures within organizations address proper prescribing and controlled substance abuse protections. In addition to addressing opioid abuse, this law also mandates that payments from biologic, pharmaceutical, medical device, and teaching hospital entities to nurse practitioners, nurse midwives, and physician assistants are tracked in a manner similar to how physicians are tracked under the Sunshine Act. Finally, as part of this ongoing effort to curb abuse, the government implemented the Eliminating Kickbacks in Recovery Act of 2018 as part of the SUPPORT Act. This law is intended to prohibit individuals from referring substance abuse patients in exchange for kickbacks to recovery homes, clinical treatment facilities, and laboratories. This provision effectively creates a tool similar to the Anti-Kickback Statute for all types of payments, not just those from the Medicare and Medicaid programs.

The Medicare Program

Medicare is a federal medical insurance program serving several groups of beneficiaries. American citizens and permanent residents qualify for Medicare if they:

- Are 65 or older
- Are entitled to Social Security or Railroad Retirement disability cash benefits for at least 24 months
- Have end-stage renal disease
- Are otherwise noncovered but elect to pay a premium for Medicare coverage

As part of the Social Security Amendments of 1965, Congress and the Johnson administration created Title XVIII of the Social Security Act: "Health Insurance for the Aged and Disabled," commonly known as Medicare. Traditional Medicare consists of two parts: hospital insurance, known as Part A, and supplementary medical insurance, known as Part B. When Medicare began on July 1, 1966, approximately 19 million people enrolled. In 2018, more than 59 million people were enrolled in Medicare.

In 2018, the federal government spent nearly $1.1 trillion on healthcare. This includes $583 billion in the Medicare program and $399 billion in the Medicaid and Children's Health Insurance Program. In short, the amount of money the government spends on healthcare is one of the largest governmental expenditures within its budget. This highlights why the government is extremely focused on implementing compliance programs to avoid wasteful government spending.

The Affordable Care Act and the Medicare program

The Patient Protection and Affordable Care Act was signed into law on March 23, 2010, changing many of the payment mechanisms under the Medicare program. First, reductions have been made regarding inpatient hospital payments. Second, there has been an across-the-board increase in payments for quality and reductions in payments for excess readmissions. Other programs that seek to change the way Medicare operates include the bundled payment programs, which provide one payment for the entire care of a patient, and accountable care organizations (ACO), which share in cost savings provided to Medicare. (ACOs are discussed in more detail later in this chapter.)

Although healthcare reform has impacted the operational and reimbursement focuses of the Medicare program, the compliance requirements remain the same.

Medical necessity

Medicare covers only those services that are reasonable and necessary for diagnosis or treatment. Medicare uses this medical necessity clause to control costs in outpatient fee-for-service settings. It empowers Medicare contractors to make medical necessity rules to determine when they will pay for individual services under Medicare.

ABNs

An advance beneficiary notice (ABN) is a form that a supplier gives to a Medicare beneficiary. ABNs inform Medicare beneficiaries that the program may not pay for an item or service used during their visit to the provider. The form allows beneficiaries to decide whether they still want to receive the item or service even if they have to pay for it out of pocket or through other insurance. Sample ABNs are available on CMS' website.

The rules for obtaining ABNs were updated in 2002, 2008, and 2011. These rules affect the Medicare carrier, intermediary, hospital, and hospice manuals, but the statutory requirements for providing ABNs have not changed.

Beneficiary Notice Initiative

Late in 2001, CMS launched the Beneficiary Notice Initiative (BNI), a webpage dedicated to helping beneficiaries understand Medicare rules. Officially, BNI provides a means to "wed consumer rights and protections with effective beneficiary communication so that beneficiaries [have] the opportunity to timely exercise of their rights and protections in a well-informed manner." The BNI also tells beneficiaries when they need to pay for a procedure and allows them to decide whether to receive the items or services "for which [they] may have to pay out of pocket or through other insurance."

Visit *www.cms.gov/Medicare/Medicare-General-Information/BNI/index* to read draft ABNs and instructions.

In most cases, providers cannot bill Medicare beneficiaries for charges that Medicare denies without obtaining a signed ABN.

Who explains coverage rules to beneficiaries?

To set forth when Medicare does not consider services medically necessary, CMS publishes national coverage determinations (NCD), and Medicare contractors publish local coverage determinations (LCD). In addition, remittance advice, sent from the fiscal intermediaries and carriers to providers, explain the reason for any denials and provide notification that Medicare does not pay for services when medical necessity criteria have not been met.

CMS and program administrators consider it their obligation to notify providers of medical necessity rules when they publish NCDs and LCDs. However, providers—not beneficiaries—receive NCDs and LCDs, so beneficiaries don't know that Medicare will not pay for a service due to lack of medical necessity. Therefore, Medicare makes providers responsible for explaining medical necessity coverage rules to beneficiaries. The limitation on liability and refund requirement clauses require beneficiaries to know that Medicare may deny a service because it does not meet the medical necessity criteria. This is why Medicare requires providers to give beneficiaries an ABN when a service may be denied for not meeting these criteria.

Ensure that beneficiaries understand that Medicare's determination is a payment determination. The treating physician ordering a service may feel that it is beneficial or necessary due to the patient's medical condition, despite Medicare's determination that it will not pay for the service. This distinction will need to be explained to beneficiaries.

Determining whether a service is medically necessary

Facilities must be able to screen for the medical necessity of a service before rendering it to Medicare patients; therefore, staff members registering patients must have access to NCDs and LCDs. A computerized method may be the best solution—in fact, many software vendors have automated this process.

Use the following process to determine the medical necessity of services:

1. Verify whether the test or service has an LCD or NCD
2. If the test or service to be performed does not have limited coverage under an NCD or LCD, proceed and perform the test or service ordered
3. If the test or service to be performed does have limited coverage under an NCD or LCD, review the signs, symptoms, or diagnosis provided by the physician and determine whether the test is considered medically necessary based on the physician's documentation

ACOs and Fraud and Abuse Laws

As discussed earlier, healthcare reform has systematized the use of ACOs, in which individual organizations band together to provide care for patients. The primary goal of an ACO is to maintain the continuum of care, increase quality, and decrease spending. In addition, Medicare ACOs may share in the savings of Medicare reimbursement. For example, if an ACO managed a population that in the previous year received $30 million in Medicare reimbursement, and in the current year the ACO is able to provide care that translates into $27 million in Medicare reimbursement, then the ACO and Medicare will both share $3 million.

Given that hospitals must adhere to the various laws discussed in this chapter, Medicare developed fraud and abuse waivers to ensure that physicians and hospitals can freely distribute shared savings received. If your organization is involved with an ACO, it is imperative that you ensure that each individual requirement is met.

Currently, CMS has issued five waivers:

1. The pre-participation waiver, which protects activities related to forming an ACO
2. The participation waiver, which protects participants in an ACO
3. The shared savings distribution waiver
4. The Stark Law waiver
5. The patient incentive waiver

Under the shared savings waiver, ACOs may use any method for distribution of savings; as long as certain requirements are met, doing so will not violate the Stark Law or Anti-Kickback Statute. In effect, the distributions do not need to be FMV or commercially reasonable. The Stark Law waiver waives potential civil monetary penalties and Anti-Kickback Statute violations with respect to arrangements between ACOs and ACO providers. However, among other requirements, to meet this waiver, the arrangement must comply with certain Stark Law exceptions.

These waivers are important with respect to any shared savings under an official Medicare ACO; however, these waivers are not available to commercial or non-Medicare ACOs. In addition, they are fairly limited in that they only apply to the shared savings distributions. Therefore, although an organization may not need savings distributions to be representative of FMV or commercially reasonable for physicians, the organization must ensure that all other aspects of the arrangement are in compliance with applicable laws.

Reference

United States Sentencing Commission (USSC). (2013). §8B2.1—Effective Compliance and Ethics Program, Chapter 8. *United States Sentencing Commission Guidelines Manual. https://guidelines.ussc.gov/gl/%C2%A78B2.1*

Chapter 4

Privacy and Security

In 1996, Congress enacted the Health Insurance Portability and Accountability Act (HIPAA), forever changing the way people and organizations interact with protected health information (PHI). The primary purpose of enacting HIPAA was to protect the security of health information and to standardize the methods by which this information is exchanged. In 2009, Congress enacted the Health Information for Economic and Clinical Health (HITECH) Act to address breach notification issues. HIPAA, as amended by HITECH, includes the Privacy Rule and the Security Rule. In 2013, the final HIPAA Omnibus Rule was issued, which implemented changes to HIPAA that were mandated by HITECH (generally referred to as the "HIPAA regulations").

The HIPAA regulations include the Privacy Rule, the Security Rule, and the Breach Notification Rule. These particular rules are discussed in detail throughout the chapter; however, compliance officers should be aware that privacy and security issues require close analysis of the laws and the particular situation presented by each issue. These rules require organizations to have a thorough understanding of the ways in which they use, store, or disclose PHI. As a preliminary issue, then compliance officers need to understand the concept of PHI.

What Is Considered PHI?

Under the HIPAA regulations, individually identifiable health information that is transmitted, accessed, or held by certain groups, in any form, is protected. In particular, PHI refers to any individually identifiable health information that can be transmitted or maintained in any form or medium. In short, if health information (including an individual's name or address) is held by a group, entity, or person covered under HIPAA, then that information is likely considered PHI so long as it could be used to identify that individual. Keep in mind that some health information can be deidentified so that it can no longer be used to identify an individual. Deidentification must meet the standard of an expert determination or the safe harbor according to which 18 identifiers have been removed and there is no residual identifiable information. If the information is deidentified, then it is no longer considered PHI, but even deidentification must follow rigorous requirements. However, not all organizations must comply with the HIPAA regulations.

To What Entities or Persons Does HIPAA Apply?

The HIPAA regulations apply to health plans, healthcare clearinghouses, and any healthcare provider who transmits health information in electronic form. These three groups are known as "covered entities" and are subject to HIPAA regulations. Each of these groups must meet the definition under the regulations. Figure 4.1 highlights examples of these entities.

FIGURE 4.1

Healthcare Provider	Healthcare Clearinghouse	Health Plans
Example: hospitals, physicians, dentists, nurse practitioners	Example: billing services, repricing companies, community health management information systems	Example: insurance entities

Healthcare providers are defined as "providers of services" such as hospitals, "providers of medical or health services" such as various physician and nurse practitioners, or any other person or organization who furnishes, bills, or is paid for healthcare in the normal course of business.

A healthcare clearinghouse means a public or private entity—including billing services, repricing companies, community health management information systems or community health information systems, and "value-added" networks and switches—that serves either of the following functions: (1) processes or facilitates nonstandard health information into a standard format or (2) receives standard health information from another entity and processes it or facilitates the processing into a nonstandard format for another entity.

Finally, a health plan is defined as an individual or group plan that provides, or pays the cost of, medical care. A health plan, as a covered entity, can include a combination of a group health plan, an insurance issuer, an HMO, or other entities as described in Section 160.103. In addition to these entities, business associates must also comply with the HIPAA regulations.

How Do the HIPAA Regulations Apply to Contractors and Subcontractors?

Although the HIPAA regulations apply to covered entities as described earlier, there are many situations in which PHI is used by those covered entities and delivered to various contractors and vendors. This can present a problem, given that even though hospitals and other entities have control over their own privacy practices, a contractor or vendor may not share those practices. To address this issue, HIPAA developed various standards and rules for those contractors, which are otherwise known as business associates.

Business associates include persons or entities that create, receive, maintain, or transmit PHI for claims processing or administration, data analysis, processing or administration, utilization review, quality assurance, patient safety activities, billing, benefit management, practice management, or repricing; or arrangements in which PHI is disclosed for legal, actuarial, accounting, data aggregation, management, administrative, accreditation, or financial services purposes.

Although this definition is expansive, it is also fluid: Whether an organization or person is considered a business associate depends on various factors. In addition, HITECH expanded the definition to include other entities that access PHI routinely. These include health information organizations, e-prescribing gateways, and vendors of personal health records.

With respect to vendors maintaining PHI, the vendor needs to do more than just receive the information and transmit it to the patient's personal health record to be considered a business associate. However, if the vendor manages a personal health record and has access to the PHI, then the vendor would be considered a business associate.

Compliance officers should recognize that the Omnibus Rule also applies to subcontractors. For example, say that a hospital contracts with a consulting firm that accesses and uses PHI. That consulting firm would be considered a business associate. However, if the consulting firm uses other subcontractors that perform functions or provide services to the business associates, and those subcontractors require access to the PHI, then the HIPAA regulations directly apply to the subcontractors. The mechanism to ensure compliance among subcontractors comes from the Security Rule, under which all business associates are required to ensure that their subcontractors comply.

Mechanism to Ensure Business Associate Compliance

In the event that a covered entity uses a contractor in a way that makes the contractor a business associate, then a business associate contract is the required method to ensure protections. Although HIPAA regulations require such an agreement, HITECH also makes business associates responsible for compliance with all of the Security Rule provisions and many of the Privacy Rule requirements.

Penalties can be imposed on a business associate for noncompliance with these rules. There are various provisions in the HIPAA regulations that must be included in these agreements, such as requiring the business associate to report use of PHI not authorized by such an agreement. A working knowledge of these agreements is important; however, deciding what should be included beyond the minimum requirements requires careful analysis of the specific engagement between the parties.

The Privacy Rule

The Privacy Rule governs the uses and disclosures of PHI. In addition, it also provides individuals with rights over their own PHI. Covered entities are required to use or disclose PHI only as authorized by the individual or the Privacy Rule itself. This might seem to limit covered entities' use and disclosure; however, there are situations under the Privacy Rule in which disclosure is permitted absent written authorization, so long as the minimum amount of PHI is disclosed.

Generally, a covered entity may disclose PHI in the following situations:

- To the individual
- For treatment, payment, or healthcare operations
- Incident to other permitted or required disclosures or uses
- With a permitted authorization
- Pursuant to an authorized agreement
- As a disclosure or use permitted in compliance with the law

Additionally, a covered entity must disclose PHI when requested by the individual. Disclosures are discussed in more detail later in this chapter; however, in general, it is important to know that some disclosures are permissible and some are required. Equally important is understanding the rights individuals have regarding their own PHI.

The Privacy Rule: Individual rights

First, individuals have a right to understand how their PHI is being used or disclosed. This notice is accomplished by providing an individual with a notice of privacy practices. The notice of privacy practices must meet specific requirements under the Privacy Rule. Although certain requirements are dependent on the uses and disclosures, some of the required provisions are highlighted in Figure 4.2.

FIGURE 4.2

Notice of Privacy Practices	
Header	"THIS NOTICE DESCRIBES HOW MEDICAL INFORMATION ABOUT YOU MAY BE USED AND DISCLOSED AND HOW YOU CAN GET ACCESS TO THIS INFORMATION. PLEASE REVIEW IT CAREFULLY."
Uses and Disclosures	Description and one example of the types of uses and disclosures that are permitted for treatment, payment, and healthcare operations
	Description of each of the other purposes permitted under the Privacy Rule without the individual's written authorization
	Statements regarding disclosures and uses that may only be made with the individual's authorization, and such authorizations can be revoked
	A description of any of the individual's other rights regarding his or her PHI

These examples highlight how the notice of privacy practices may be expanded depending on the level of use or types of disclosures. Covered entities are also required to make a good-faith effort to obtain a written acknowledgment that the individual received a copy of the notice of privacy practices. The only exception for making a good-faith effort may occur in emergency treatment situations.

Beyond the notice of privacy practices, individuals also have a right to access their PHI. In particular, individuals have a right of access to inspect and obtain a copy of their PHI within a designated record set. Certain exceptions include psychotherapy notes and information in anticipation for use in a civil, criminal, or administrative proceeding.

FIGURE 4.3
HIPAA Definition of Designated Record Set
A designated record set is: • A group of records maintained by or for a covered entity • The medical records and billing records about individuals maintained by or for a covered healthcare provider • The enrollment, payment, claims adjudication, and case or medical management record systems maintained by or for a health plan • Used, in whole or in part, by or for the covered entity to make decisions about individuals

Individuals also have a right to request amendments to their PHI located within the designated record set. The covered entity may deny this request if the PHI was not created by the covered entity (so long as the originator of the PHI is available to act on the request), the PHI is not part of the designated record set, the PHI is not available for inspection, or the covered entity determines that the PHI is accurate and complete. However, among other requirements, a denial must be given in writing and provided to the individual in a timely manner.

Additionally, individuals have a right to restrict disclosures and uses of their PHI. This right pertains only to situations in which uses and disclosures of PHI are made for healthcare operations, treatment, and payment. Only in limited circumstances, though, is a covered entity obligated to restrict such uses and disclosures.

Finally, individuals have a right to request that PHI be communicated in a different manner or at a different location and a right to receive an accounting of specific disclosures within six years of the request. Although individuals have rights with respect to PHI, covered entities must ensure that in all situations of use or disclosure, only the minimum amount of PHI necessary is used or disclosed.

The Privacy Rule: Minimum necessary

Each of these individual disclosures has specific requirements, but for many of them, the compliance department should ensure that only the minimum necessary information is disclosed. As mentioned earlier, this requirement means that covered entities "must make reasonable efforts to limit protected health information to the minimum necessary to accomplish the intended purpose of the use, disclosure, or request." This does not apply to the following situations:

1. Disclosures to or requests by a healthcare provider for treatment
2. Some uses or disclosures made to the individual
3. Uses or disclosures that the individual authorizes
4. Many uses or disclosures required by law

The Privacy Rule: Disclosures that are permitted absent written authorization

Under the Privacy Rule, there are instances in which disclosures are permitted without patient authorization. First and foremost, any disclosures made to individuals regarding their own PHI are permissible without their authorization. This allows covered entities to freely disclose and discuss PHI with those individuals without risk. There is also a catchall provision allowing disclosure for treatment, payment, or healthcare operations.

Treatment is defined as the provision, coordination, or management of healthcare and related services by one or more healthcare providers, including the coordination or management of healthcare by a healthcare provider with a third party. It also includes consultation between healthcare providers relating to a patient or the referral of a patient for healthcare from one healthcare provider to another.

The payment exception includes activities undertaken by a health plan to obtain premiums or to resolve coverage issues or actions taken by a healthcare provider or health plan in obtaining reimbursement.

Examples of exceptions under this definition include determining coverage under a plan and billing or collection activities.

Healthcare operations include the following:

- Quality assessment and improvement activities
- Patient safety activities
- Business operations related to treatment and payments
- Issues relating to training, evaluation, licensing, and accreditation
- Medical reviews, legal services, and auditing functions
- Contracts related to health insurance
- The sale of a covered entity to another covered entity

Although the above are the primary instances in which disclosures are permitted without patient authorization, there are other exceptions that apply to covered entities. For example, if a disclosure is made incident to a use or disclosure that is otherwise permitted, then patient authorization is not required. Covered entities also may use PHI for the purpose of fundraising so long as the information is related to demographic data or the dates of healthcare provided to an individual. Finally, there are exceptions involving deidentified data, uses and disclosures that require an opportunity to agree or object, and a disclosure to an entity when there is a HIPAA-compliant business associate agreement.

Generally, if a use or disclosure does not fit within one of those exceptions, then written authorization is required from the individual.

Uses and disclosures requiring authorization by the individual

Receiving written authorization from an individual can be problematic given the resources and time it may take to receive it. Nonetheless, the Privacy Rule does designate four different instances in which written authorization is mandatory. They include marketing, the sale of PHI, the use and disclosure of psychotherapy notes, and anything not permitted by the Privacy Rule.

The term "marketing" is not a catchall, however. For face-to-face communications made by a covered entity to an individual, authorization is not required. In addition, if the marketing is a promotional gift of nominal value provided by the covered entity, then authorization is not required. That said, any other communication to encourage an individual to use a product or service requires disclosure if PHI is being disclosed. Therefore, compliance officers should pay close attention to any disclosures of PHI by the marketing department to ensure compliance with this rule.

Another concern relates to the disclosure of PHI through its sale. The Privacy Rule requires written authorization for any direct or indirect remuneration received for PHI. In addition, any such authorization must state that the disclosure will result in remuneration to the covered entity. Exceptions to this rule include certain selling of PHI for the purpose of research, public health, or treatment and payment. Finally, authorization is required for any use or disclosure of psychotherapy notes with the exception of carrying out treatment, payment, or healthcare options in limited circumstances.

As you can see, although the situations discussed above have various exceptions, more often than not it is likely that a written authorization will be required. The Privacy Rule contains specific requirements for any authorization form or document.

Written authorization elements

To begin, each written authorization must contain the following elements:

1. A description of the information to be used or disclosed that identifies such information in a specific and meaningful manner
2. The name of the person or group that is making the authorization
3. The name of the person, group, or entity to whom the covered entity will disclose the information
4. A statement such as "at the request of the individual" or similar language that describes each purpose of the requested use or disclosure
5. An expiration date or event for the purpose of the use or disclosure (if there is no expiration date or event, then "none" may suffice)
6. The signature of the individual and date (if a personal representative is signing on the individual's behalf, then a description of the authority must be included)

In addition to these core elements, written authorizations must contain the individual's right to revoke, how the individual can revoke the authorization, and one of the following: (1) the exceptions to the right to revoke and how the individual may revoke or (2) notices required as it pertains to privacy practices.

The Security Rule

Although the Privacy Rule applies to various types of health information, the Security Rule applies only to electronic protected health information (ePHI). The major goal of the Security Rule is to ensure that proper safeguards are in place for the storing, maintaining, and transmitting of ePHI. The safeguards concerning ePHI under the Security Rule apply to covered entities and business associates. Above all, the Security Rule safeguards apply to your organization only if you are a covered entity or business associate and your organization stores, maintains, or transmits ePHI.

Reasonable and appropriate security measures

Under the Security Rule, there are various administrative, physical, and technical safeguards that can be implemented. However, the Security Rule also is flexible in that an analysis is necessary to determine the appropriate implementation specifications needed for various environments.

Organizations are allowed to use a similarly flexible approach to implement these standards. Each organization's analysis should take into account the size of the organization; the technical, hardware, and software security infrastructure; the costs of the security measures; and the probability of risks to ePHI. Compliance officers should also be aware that certain specifications are required while others are addressable. In all cases, the covered entity must perform an assessment and implement the specification if it is reasonable and appropriate; if it is not, the entity must document why it is not implementing the specification and provide an equivalent alternative.

The Security Rule standards

The Security Rule's safeguards have standards and implementation specifications. Any analysis of the implementation specifications requires close scrutiny of the terms and language. However, the standards for each safeguard help organizations understand the goal when implementing such a safeguard for the purpose of protecting ePHI. Under the administrative safeguards, organizations must adhere to the following standards to comply with the Security Rule:

- Security management process: Implement policies and procedures to prevent, detect, contain, and correct security violations
- Assigned security responsibility: Assign a leader who is responsible for such policies and procedures
- Workforce security: Implement policies and procedures to ensure appropriate access to ePHI
- Information access management: Implement policies and procedures to authorize access to ePHI

- Security awareness and training: Implement a training program for the entire workforce
- Security incident procedures: Implement policies and procedures to address security incidents
- Contingency plan: Establish a plan for emergency occurrences, such as system failures or natural disasters
- Evaluation: Perform periodical technical and nontechnical evaluations

Under the physical safeguards, organizations must adhere to the following standards to comply with the Security Rule:

- Facility access controls: Implement policies and procedures to limit access to systems and facilities
- Workstation use: Address proper functions to be performed at specific workstations or groups of workstations
- Workstation security: Physical safeguards should restrict access to authorized users
- Device and media controls: Implement policies and procedures relating to the receipt or removal of hardware and media that contain ePHI

Under the technical safeguards, organizations must adhere to the following standards to comply with the Security Rule:

- Access control: Implement policies and procedures to limit access to only those persons or software allowed access under the Security Rule
- Audit controls: Implement mechanisms to record and examine information system activity with respect to ePHI
- Integrity: Implement policies and procedures to protect against alteration or destruction issues
- Person or entity authentication: Verification of person seeking access to ePHI
- Transmission security: Guard against unauthorized access to ePHI

All covered entities and business associates must implement such policies and procedures to comply with the Security Rule. Organizations should be mindful of the reasonable and appropriate standard when it comes to implementation specifications, and all documentation required must be maintained for six years from the date of its creation or when it was last in effect, whichever is later.

Generally, the safeguard standards and the implementation specifications require a clear understanding of your organization's information system infrastructure. In addition to the issues covered under the Security Rule, the HIPAA regulations also require policies and procedures for notifying individuals when a breach has occurred.

Breach Notification

The Breach Notification Rule requires covered entities and business associates to implement notification policies and procedures in the event that a breach of unsecured PHI is discovered. Under the rule, unsecured PHI is defined as PHI that "is not rendered unusable, unreadable, or indecipherable to unauthorized persons through the use of a technology or methodology specified by the Secretary" of the U.S. Department of Health and Human Services (HHS).

As an initial concern, compliance officers should be diligent in understanding how PHI can be secured to avoid breach issues. Nevertheless, there are many instances in which a breach may have occurred, and understanding the requirements for when a breach is considered to have taken place can help your organization develop the proper processes.

Breach notification: What is a breach and when does it occur?

In order for organizations to effectively implement policies and procedures regarding the breach of PHI, it is necessary to carefully analyze the definition of a breach under the rule and when a breach may occur. Under the rule, a breach means the "acquisition, access, use, or disclosure of protected health information in a manner not permitted ... which compromises the security or privacy of the protected health information." This definition provides guidance as to the definition of a breach but still leaves questions about when a breach may occur. Is an employee of a covered entity able to create a breach under the rule? Is an inadvertent disclosure considered a breach?

The Breach Notification Rule provides some insight into these questions. First, a breach does include acquisition of, access to, or use of PHI by a member of the workforce or a person acting under the authority of a covered entity or business associate if such a "breach" is made in good faith and within the scope of the person's authority and does not result in further use or disclosure. Second, inadvertent disclosures by a person who is authorized to access PHI to another authorized person, without further use or disclosure of the information, would not be considered a breach.

With respect to the timing of discovery, an organization is considered to have knowledge of a breach once it is known or should have been known if the organization had been exercising reasonable diligence.

Nevertheless, organizations should first analyze whether an alleged breach is actually considered a breach under the definition.

Breach notification: What should be done when a breach occurs?

Once a risk assessment has been considered along with other applicable factors and the organization has determined that a breach has occurred, the Breach Notification Rule requires certain disclosures and notifications. First, the covered entity must notify each individual whose unsecured PHI has been or is reasonably believed to have been involved in a breach. Such notification should occur without unreasonable delay and in no case later than 60 calendar days after the discovery of the breach.

Each such notification must include the following:

- A brief description of what happened, including the date of breach and discovery
- A description of the types of PHI breached
- Steps individuals should take to protect themselves from harm
- A brief description of the internal investigation
- Any contact procedures for questions, including a toll-free telephone number, email address, website, or postal address

Written notice is required unless there is insufficient contact information or the situation is considered more emergent.

In the event that a breach involves more than 500 individuals of a state or jurisdiction, media outlets in the area must be notified. Although there are different standards with respect to notifying HHS of a breach depending on the number of individuals involved, in all cases, HHS must be notified in the manner specified on its website. This includes potentially notifying HHS concurrently with the notice to affected individuals or on an annual basis.

Breach notification: Business associates

Many organizations may experience possible breaches with respect to their business associates. Although business associates must adhere to many of the same Privacy and Security Rules as covered entities, their breach notification process is slightly different. First, business associates must notify the covered entity without unreasonable delay and not later than 60 days from the date of discovery. However, organizations may negotiate a shorter period of time under their business associate agreements. In all cases, covered entities should carefully analyze the relationship with the business associate to ensure that the date of discovery by the business associate is not imputed to the covered entity.

Penalties and Enforcement

The penalties under the HIPAA regulations can be severe. First, although individuals are unable to sue a covered entity for a violation, they may notify the HHS Office of Civil Rights (OCR) of their complaint. Once a complaint of a violation has occurred, the OCR along with that state's attorney general may impose civil penalties ranging from $100 to $50,000 per violation. Second, violations under HITECH can lead to additional violations in the amounts of $25,000–$1,500,000.

Finally, there are additional civil monetary penalties should an organization be found to be acting in willful neglect of the law. Each penalty is dependent on the level of culpability, ranging from not knowing to willful neglect and not taking corrective action.

Currently, each violation can result in a penalty between $100 and $50,000, but the aggregate amount is a maximum of $1,500,000. Nevertheless, this does not allow organizations to cap any and all violations. HHS has noted that a covered entity or business associate may be subject to multiple violations of up to the $1,500,000 cap for each violation, which would result in a total penalty of more than $1,500,000.

Other Privacy and Cybersecurity Laws

Recently, both state and federal governments have become more involved with implementing new cybersecurity and privacy laws. Although many of these laws are applicable to data generally, these laws still apply to information that is transmitted within a health system. Therefore, as a compliance officer, you must ensure that your organization has addressed cybersecurity threats and state or local laws.

Cybersecurity Staffing and Committee

Organizations should develop internal cybersecurity experts, including an information security officer, and a cybersecurity program. The information security officer will be charged with analyzing and assessing all information threats from various software and programs that interact with an organization's systems. For example, if an organization seeks to implement new telehealth software, the information security officer should review the software from a security perspective. The cybersecurity program should have either a direct connection or a dotted line connection to the compliance officer. This relationship is typically dictated by the departments currently developed within an organization. For example, if an organization has an established cybersecurity department separate from compliance, a dotted line is more likely to exist. It is worth noting that many organizations might define their information protection as a cybersecurity program or an information security program.

Organizations should hire an information security officer rather than splitting these duties between several existing officers. Information security is complex and changes rapidly; therefore, it requires not only dedicated support but also expertise. An information security officer should have experience working in the field and be dedicated to maintaining ongoing professional education.

A mature cybersecurity program should include a committee that analyzes and addresses information security issues. This may or may not include true PHI issues; however, it is critically important that a group of stakeholders be able to address these complex issues for an organization.

The committee should be composed of multiple departments that interact with information and security issues. Those include compliance, information technology, finance, legal, and operations. Stakeholders from these departments should be included because each of these departments is able to assist in large-scale changes across an organization, and they are not siloed in one department. The individuals selected should have expertise or interest in cybersecurity.

Recent Developments

As discussed earlier in this chapter, there has been significant movement in both state and federal law in regard to privacy and cybersecurity issues. For example, in 2019, New York implemented the SHIELD Act. This act expanded breach notification laws to include other information, such as passwords and email addresses. It also placed breach notification requirements on all businesses and individuals and created data security requirements based upon the size of the business. In California, the California Consumer Privacy Act was enacted in 2018. This sweeping law placed additional requirements on how consumers control data collected by the businesses with which they interact.

The SHIELD Act and the California Consumer Privacy Act are only two examples of the dozens of state privacy and cybersecurity laws that have gone into effect recently. With this in mind, it's more critical than ever that the compliance department have a fundamental understanding of the applicable laws in the state or states in which your organization operates. Although in healthcare, privacy and security efforts are often focused on PHI and data in medical records, prudent compliance officers must evaluate risks beyond the medical record, as significant regulatory changes are likely to continue to occur for all forms of data.

Conclusion

Organizations should be mindful of state laws regarding privacy, security, and breach notification. Most states have laws pertaining to privacy issues, and HIPAA does not preempt all state laws. Therefore, it is imperative that each organization properly analyze its individual state laws with respect to any type of PHI. The HIPAA regulations have many nuances; however, a base working knowledge of the applicable security issues will help your organization understand the questions to ask and the actions to take. In addition, ensure that your organization continues to focus on all forms of data, cybersecurity, and overall information security.

An organization should approach PHI and all data strategically and work to develop processes and procedures that not only adhere to the law but also allow it to work more effectively.

Chapter 5

Revenue Cycle Compliance

All compliance programs should include processes targeted to the revenue cycle, with a specific focus on coding and billing compliance. The revenue cycle is key to the organization's financial health but also represents serious risks. To create an effective revenue cycle compliance program, it is imperative that the organization understand the unique compliance risks associated with coding, billing, and reimbursement. In recent years, government agencies such as the Office of Inspector General (OIG) and the Centers for Medicare & Medicaid Services (CMS) have put substantial focus on payment issues including upcoding, lack of documentation, and billing for services not performed.

As a compliance officer, you must be a key partner in and resource for the revenue cycle. It will be your duty to provide guidance, ensuring that revenue cycle processes comply with all applicable regulations and best practices. The revenue cycle is complex, with many interconnected functions. To effectively manage revenue cycle compliance risks, you will need to go beyond a general understanding of your organization's revenue cycle structure and key revenue cycle principles.

Compliance Risks in the Revenue Cycle and Coding Processes

Healthcare organizations are obligated by several regulations, such as the False Claims Act (FCA), to ensure that their payment mechanisms and billing systems are accurate. Failing to comply with these regulations can result in serious consequences, ranging from substantial monetary penalties to accusations of criminal wrongdoing. In addition, poor billing and payment systems present a basic financial risk to an organization. Inaccurate bills can result in underpayments as easily as overpayments and will impact data used to forecast the organization's financial performance. Understanding these risks will help compliance officers better communicate the need for a high-functioning revenue cycle compliance program.

There are specific state and federal laws that can result in penalties for inappropriate coding and billing. Other chapters in this book discuss some of the major federal regulations, including the FCA, the Health Care Fraud Statute, and the Anti-Kickback Statute, in more detail. In addition to the state and federal laws that mandate appropriate coding and billing practices, organizations have numerous contracts with third-party payers. These contracts typically include coding and billing requirements and charge the provider organization with managing a compliance program.

If it is found that an organization has been billing inappropriately, the penalties can range from repayment to criminal liability, if there was intent to defraud the government. Although most billing issues are technical in nature, all represent a compliance risk that must be mitigated. Therefore, the compliance officer must have a robust understanding of these risks, as well as the technical nature of billing and coding processes.

The Revenue Cycle Process

The revenue cycle begins when a patient presents for treatment and continues through the patient's treatment to payment. In short, the revenue cycle is the point A to point Z of patient service. In general, most compliance staff might not have an in depth understanding of the revenue cycle. Although much of this chapter focuses on billing and coding, the overall revenue cycle process has other components that create risk for all organizations. Therefore, a compliance officer must be aware of each step in the process and its potential risks.

One of the first steps in the revenue cycle is patient registration, where the patient's demographic information is entered into the organization's records and his or her ability to pay is verified. Each patient is identified based upon their eligibility to pay through an insurance company, a government healthcare program, or directly. A patient's eligibility for financial assistance, charity care, or enrollment in government healthcare programs may also be assessed. This step generally involves exchanging a significant amount of data between the patient and the organization. This includes demographic and payment data, such as the patient's insurance identification number, and information about the services expected to be rendered (e.g., a lab test or presurgical assessment). This step in the revenue cycle is extremely important for generating revenue, as something as simple as a spelling error when entering a patient's name can lead to delays in reimbursement. From a compliance perspective, this step is also a critical point for a variety of compliance risks. For example, if a patient is incorrectly billed, this could lead to a violation of the FCA or, at a minimum, negatively impact your ability to track claims appropriately.

The next step in the revenue cycle is collecting copayments owed at the point of service, coding the claim, and submitting the claim for the services provided. There are a number of compliance risks at this step. First, collection of copayments can present a compliance risk if an organization is systematically choosing who to collect copayments from and others who they do not collect from. This can result in various levels of liability. For example, by selectively choosing which patients to collect copayments from, you run the risk of violating various anti-discrimination laws applicable to federal healthcare programs. In addition, in the event that a copayment is required, if an organization is not collecting copayments, then it is possible that there is risk under patient inducement regulations. In short, an organization could be accused of waiving these payments to induce patients to receive more services. Further, the actual coding of the claim is extremely critical to any compliance program.

With respect to coding, there are various risks to keep in mind. As mentioned earlier in this chapter, incorrect coding can result in liability under several federal and state laws as well as under the terms of contracts with commercial insurers. However, the complexity of coding is often understated. This is because payers might have different coding, documentation, billing, and even clinical requirements for the same service. These requirements can become highly complex in practice, particularly if several payers have markedly different requirements, and it is often challenging to educate staff on them. Therefore, coding will be a critical area within any compliance program, and the compliance officer is often charged with ensuring that coding is appropriate and correct.

Finally, the next steps within revenue cycle customarily include collecting any additional payments and following up on denials of claims. In general, specific revenue cycle staff are assigned to manage denied claims, including tracking denials by type and payer and filing appeals. A compliance officer should understand the various reasons for which a claim might be denied. Appropriate review and auditing of denied claims is a necessary component of revenue cycle monitoring. These offer an opportunity for an organization to understand whether the services that they are providing are appropriate based upon the code. Denied claims are a good indicator of overall revenue cycle performance and can be used to identify errors that occur earlier in the revenue cycle, such as coding errors or insufficient documentation of medical necessity. Therefore, review and auditing of denied claims is a necessary component of monitoring revenue cycle compliance.

Coding Compliance

Coding errors can occur for many reasons. A coder might not be aware of a recent code change and, therefore, might use an incorrect code. Or perhaps the claim is for a service newly offered by the organization and the coding team does not yet have sufficient guidance. Or the claim may be for complex services and diagnoses, such as sepsis, that are inherently challenging to code correctly. Nevertheless, correctly coding each claim is critical, as even a simple error can result in a false claim.

Due to the complexity of coding, compliance programs must have adequate safeguards in place. Although a major focus of a compliance program should be claims submitted to Medicare, Medicaid, and other government healthcare programs, claims submitted to private payers cannot be left out. Organizations should have processes and policies in place to effectively mitigate all risks and ensure compliance with government and private payers' requirements.

First, a compliance program should ensure that individuals can detect any specific problems. This should include monitoring and feedback processes from individuals involved in functions that create compliance risks. For example, random chart audits should be a routine method of ensuring coding compliance and detecting specific problems. Although random chart audits can be time-consuming, if there is a known issue or a new service has been introduced, they are worth considering. For a new service, a proper audit should include evaluating multiple factors, including the code itself and what guidelines are associated with that code as well as the clinical documentation to support appropriate use of the code. Along with random chart audits, the compliance department should explore other options to detect coding and documentation weaknesses, including manual and software processes.

It isn't sufficient to simply detect that an error is occurring. Organizations must have processes to correct errors and compliance issues and to prevent them from happening again. For example, if an organization is performing a chart audit, for any issues that are found, the claim should be sent to the health information management department, in which coding and billing are typically housed, to be corrected.

Revenue Cycle Metrics to Understand

Revenue cycle metrics, even those that are not driven specifically by regulations, allow organizations to set best practices for efficiently billing and collecting payment. A compliance officer must be cognizant of these metrics and the best practices they support to effectively partner with the revenue cycle.

Each organization's revenue cycle may have organization-specific best practices and metrics it monitors, but many are industrywide. For example, most revenue cycle departments monitor their days in accounts receivable (A/R) and strive to keep them below a certain threshold. A/R is how long it takes an organization to receive payment for services provided. By ensuring that accounts move appropriately through A/R, the revenue cycle helps to ensure that timely claim filing deadlines are met.

Other notable revenue cycle metrics are the net collection rate and the percent of accounts in A/R over a certain number of days. Knowing the percent of accounts in A/R allows an organization to assess how quickly they can collect payment. A net collection rate is the amount an organization collects based upon what it is able or eligible to collect. Consider a scenario in which a patient is charged $100 and the organization collects $95. In this case, your net collections rate would be 95%.

Education

The compliance department should have an active education program for all individuals involved with the revenue cycle with training sessions specific to revenue cycle topics. This annual training should consider broader issues as well as more unique and nuanced issues. For example, education on broader issues could include information on how to analyze and approach new services and what compliance looks at to determine risks. Such information gives staff a fundamental understanding of risk assessment. Organizations are advised to consider role-specific compliance training with modules tailored to specific revenue cycle departments as well as documentation compliance training for clinical staff.

New and urgent revenue cycle compliance concerns should be communicated through newsletters sent to staff, issue-specific training, and other methods, such as presentations at interdepartmental meetings.

Above all, the education program should be robust and proactive due to the constantly changing nature of the revenue cycle. A federal audit or investigation will focus on whether the organization has proactive processes in place. This includes proactively monitoring, educating, and partnering with departments to identify compliance risks. If an organization has deficiencies in these areas, that may give federal auditors or investigators the impression that the organization lacks an effective compliance program.

Education on coding and billing practices

Claims are coded using several distinct code sets. ICD-10-Procedure Coding System (ICD-10-PCS) is used for procedural coding—that is, surgical, medical, or diagnostic interventions. ICD-10-Clinical Modification (ICD-10-CM) is used to code diagnoses and reason for visit. These two codes sets are maintained by CMS and the National Center for Health Statistics. The Current Procedural Terminology (CPT®) code set is used to report outpatient and office procedures to payers; this code set is proprietary and is maintained by the American Medical Association (AMA). The Healthcare Common Procedure Coding System (HCPCS) code set consists of two code sets: HCPCS Level I, or CPT codes, and HCPCS Level II. HCPCS Level II codes are used to report medical devices, supplies, medications, and other items and services.

Generally, coding and billing rules are set by statute and CMS regulations, such as the agency's annual prospective payment system final rules or quarterly code updates. These publications may introduce new codes or delete codes and define coding requirements and guidelines. However, a great deal of information on appropriate use of codes, accepted billing, claim edits, and documentation requirements is published by CMS, as well as other federal and state agencies, in transmittals. Some of these transmittals are addressed to provider organizations, whereas others are addressed to the Medicare Administrative Contractors (MAC) who are responsible for processing claims.

In addition, the American Hospital Association releases coding guidance in its *Coding Clinics,* and the AMA publishes updates and information for its proprietary CPT code set.

Private payers also release billing and coding guidance. Each payer may release updates in a different way: some payers publish updates on their websites, and others may send updates to provider organizations. If updates are sent to the provider organization, different payers may send the updates to different departments or individuals.

All of these resources change regularly and must be reviewed frequently. Monitoring government and private payer coding and billing updates can be time-consuming; however, each organization is responsible for ensuring that its practices are current and compliant. Although as a compliance officer you may not be expected to have detailed knowledge of coding and billing, you should have an understanding of the fundamentals and keep informed of changes. The following is a list of CMS resources that should be regularly reviewed:

- *www.cms.gov/Regulations-and-Guidance/Guidance/Transmittals*
- *www.cms.gov/Regulations-and-Guidance/Regulations-and-Guidance*
- *www.cms.gov/Medicare/Medicare-Contracting/Medicare-Administrative-Contractors/MedicareAdministrativeContractors*

A compliance officer should review payer updates and stay abreast of coding changes. Depending on the size of the organization, if there is a dedicated coding department, the compliance officer should ensure that he or she is in regular communication with the coding department to be notified of coding changes. If the organization does not have a robust coding team, the compliance officer will need to rely on professional resources to stay abreast of coding updates and changes.

Policies and Procedures

Clear policies and procedures on key risk areas are the foundation of any compliance program. For the revenue cycle, key policies and procedures include coding, billing, documentation, and the chargemaster, as well as medical necessity and scope of practice. Generally, an organization will be reimbursed only for medically necessary services. Ensuring that services are medically necessary and that the determination is clearly documented in the medical record are key responsibilities for revenue cycle functions, such as utilization review and clinical documentation improvement. In addition, scope of practice rules, both federal and state/local, impact how certain services are coded and billed and entail specific documentation requirements.

An organization that lacks these policies and procedures runs the risk of an audit uncovering that it does not have an effective compliance program. For example, if an organization is audited and forced to repay certain claims due to lack of policies, procedures, and education on medical necessity, this would represent an ongoing risk not being effectively addressed by the compliance department. If there are further investigations by the government, a lack of policies and procedures can be a compounding factor.

A compliance officer will need to collaborate with revenue cycle departments to develop and oversee policies and procedures. This can be a time-consuming task, so it is recommended that organizations take a proactive approach.

In addition to those broad areas, an organization should create a billing and standard conduct policy. This policy should maintain expectations related to billing practices for all staff that are involved in the process. This policy should maintain expectations related to billing practices and should be distributed to all revenue cycle staff. Any and all additional policies and standard operating procedures should also be incorporated into revenue cycle policies and procedures.

People, Processes, and Infrastructure

Policies and procedures will support compliance in the revenue cycle, but it's equally important to ensure that the right personnel and committees are in place. Without these key individuals and structures in place, revenue cycle compliance will not have the appropriate oversight, and risks may not be properly addressed.

Organizations seeking to develop stronger billing and coding compliance programs should first ensure that the compliance staff working in these areas understand billing and coding practices. It is not uncommon for large health systems to employ compliance staff that focus specifically on billing and coding compliance. Depending on the size of the organization, one individual in the compliance department can be assigned to this task or a group of individuals might have responsibility for this oversight.

In addition to dedicated oversight in the compliance department, organizations should have a revenue cycle compliance committee. The value, role, and recommended makeup of the revenue cycle compliance committee will be discussed in more detail later in this chapter.

Key Strategies to Mitigate Risk

All organizations need to focus on key opportunities for improvement. When considering billing and coding compliance, there are a few different areas on which a compliance department should focus to ensure that risk mitigation is active and occurring.

Leadership/committee structure

First, a revenue cycle compliance committee should be established. The committee will address day-to-day compliance issues and may include a special subcommittee dedicated to billing and coding. The committee should include key stakeholders from compliance, coding, reimbursement, revenue cycle, and clinical leaders and should communicate any compliance concerns to a board-level compliance committee. Committee meetings should be held on a regular schedule, stated in the committee's statement of work, rather than on an *ad hoc* basis.

Along with day-to-day compliance issues, the committee should discuss implementation of new services and other initiatives, as well as create a platform for internal assessment and monitoring activities. This group could also discuss emerging issues and root cause analysis for specific compliance issues that have arisen in the revenue cycle.

New services and equipment

All new services, equipment, and treatments should be reviewed or a plan created to review how they might impact billing and coding. This review includes legal and compliance as well as finance and IT teams. By reviewing these new services with multiple stakeholders, the teams will be able to develop policies and procedures for them and launch a pilot program prior to going live. In addition, when a new service is implemented, the organization can establish an auditing and monitoring schedule for coding, billing, and documentation compliance.

Risk-based auditing and monitoring

Another effective strategy for identifying and preventing revenue cycle risks is to create a risk-based auditing and monitoring plan. The criteria can be planned on an annual basis and may be based on the activities and focus of external entities. For example, the OIG's *Work Plan* describes key audit areas for the federal government. You may also look at other areas such as code updates or audits conducted by third-party payers. By creating a risk-based auditing and monitoring plan, you can effectively create an annual program strictly based upon identifying and preventing issues.

In addition, the compliance department should establish event-reporting thresholds so that appropriate investigations can occur and corrective action plans can be developed within specific time frames.

Conclusion

The revenue cycle is an extremely complex process and one that presents a significant number of compliance risks. The compliance officer holds a unique role in the revenue cycle and must work closely with revenue cycle leaders to ensure that both departments have a mutual understanding of their responsibilities and obligations. The nuances of revenue cycle compliance mean that the compliance officer must be familiar with key concepts and understand how the revenue cycle supports the organization. At the same time, the compliance officer must promote the compliance function within the revenue cycle and ensure that all staff within the revenue cycle understand how compliance guides and supports their work.

The compliance department is charged with helping the revenue cycle interpret regulations and identify auditing and monitoring priorities. To support this goal, the compliance department should create resources, assist with the development of policies and procedures, and be involved in general and specific compliance training. As is discussed in other chapters in this book, the compliance department may consider using tracking and monitoring tools to ensure that training is completed and staff acknowledge that they have received updates.

Compliance and revenue cycle staff must be updated on key changes in regulations as well as on the types of services that their organization offers. Designated individuals should be responsible for monitoring payer updates and alerting compliance and revenue cycle leaders of any changes.

Both the compliance and revenue cycle departments must be adequately staffed. Any compliance staff dedicated to the revenue cycle must have a more than general understanding of revenue cycle processes.

Finally, the compliance officer should focus on creating key strategies to identify revenue cycle compliance risks. Continued focus on these key areas will allow your billing and coding compliance program to strengthen.

Chapter 6

Fair Market Value and Commercial Reasonableness

Compliance officers are typically tasked with evaluating compensation arrangements and providing oversight to ensure that all financial arrangements with referral sources are both fair market value and commercially reasonable. This can be a challenging task, as there are frequently competing factors in the evaluation of a financial arrangement. Such factors may include the demand by the referral source, general market conditions (i.e., supply and demand of the service), the business objectives of your client, and benchmark data or other general market indications of relative value for the financial arrangement. Compliance officers will need to weigh each of these factors and assist their organizations in developing sufficient supporting documentation to prove that financial arrangements are both fair market value and commercially reasonable.

Fair Market Value Defined

According to the Stark Law, fair market value is defined as follows (CMS, 2004):

> *Fair market value means the value in arm's-length transactions, consistent with the general market value. 'General market value' means the price that an asset would bring as the result of bona fide bargaining between well-informed buyers and sellers who are not otherwise in a position to generate business for the other party, or the compensation that would be included in a service agreement as the result of bona fide bargaining between well-informed parties to the agreement who are not otherwise in a position to generate business for the other party, on the date of acquisition of the asset or at the time of the service agreement.*
>
> *Usually, the fair market price is the price at which bona fide sales have been consummated for assets of like type, quality, and quantity in a particular market at the time of acquisition, or the compensation that has been included in bona fide service agreements with comparable terms at the time of the agreement, where the price or compensation has not been determined in any manner that takes into account the volume or value of anticipated or actual referrals.*
>
> *With respect to rentals and leases described in § 411.357(a), (b), and (l) (as to equipment leases only), 'fair market value' means the value of rental property for general commercial purposes (not taking into account its intended use). In the case of a lease of space, this value may not be adjusted to reflect the additional value the prospective lessee or lessor would attribute to the proximity or convenience to the lessor when the lessor is a potential source of patient referrals to the lessee. For purposes of this definition, a rental payment does not take into account intended use if it takes into account costs incurred by the lessor in developing or upgrading the property or maintaining the property or its improvements.*

Although the Stark Law defines fair market value, no such definition exists under the Anti-Kickback Statute. Therefore, you can use the Stark Law's definition as guidance when conducting an Anti-Kickback Statute review.

There is a formal body of knowledge and professional standards that governs the appraisal practice for real estate and business valuations. However, there is no current body of knowledge or standards for compensation valuations. Thus, for each compensation arrangement with which you are assisting your client, you will need to assemble documentation that you believe is reasonable and sufficient to justify the compensation paid.

As noted earlier in the definition of fair market value under the Stark Law, fair market value will be determined "on the date of acquisition of the asset or at the time of the service agreement." Therefore, as long as the term of the financial arrangement is reasonable, fair market value will be determined at the inception of the financial arrangement even if market conditions change subsequently.

Fair market value is an important compliance issue for compliance officers, as several settlements, investigations, and *qui tam* cases have involved issues of fair market value with referring physicians and entities.

Commercial Reasonableness Defined

The U.S. Department of Health and Human Services (HHS) has defined commercial reasonableness as "a sensible, prudent business agreement, from the perspective of the particular parties involved, even in the absence of any potential referrals" (*U.S. vs. SCCI,* 2004). Under the Stark Law Phase II final rule, commercial reasonableness is defined as follows: "An arrangement will be considered 'commercially reasonable' in the absence of referrals if the arrangement would make commercial sense if entered into by a reasonable entity of similar type and size and a reasonable physician (or family member or group practice) of similar scope and specialty, even if there were no potential DHS referrals" (*U.S. v. Tuomey*, 2013).

Determining whether a financial arrangement is commercially reasonable is separate and distinct from a fair market value determination. By way of example, it may be fair market value to pay a cardiothoracic surgeon $300 an hour for clinical services, but it would not be commercially reasonable to pay that physician $300 an hour to mow the hospital's grass. Although the compensation may be fair market value *based upon the physician's specialty,* the grass mowing would not be commercially reasonable based upon the compensation paid. Another example is to pay a physician for medical director, administrative, or consulting services when the services do not require the services of a physician.

Commercial reasonableness is definitely a challenge with respect to administrative and consulting services, such as medical directorships or a paid physician consultant for a device manufacturer or pharmaceutical entity. To ensure that administrative services are commercially reasonable, you will need to make sure that the tasks assigned to the physician are needed by the hospital and that a physician of his or her particular specialty needs to perform such tasks. By way of example, you may need an orthopedic surgeon to be the orthopedic surgery medical director, but you may not need that surgeon to serve on a committee to evaluate your electronic health record program, even though a physician's participation is essential. The service of a physician may be commercially reasonable, but the compensation based on an orthopedic surgeon's clinical hourly rate may not be commercially reasonable.

The government's expert witness in the case of *U.S. v. SCCI Hospital Houston* provided observations regarding commercial reasonableness, including 1) the arrangement should be essential to the hospital's operations; 2) if the arrangement is clinical in nature, it must be related to meeting patient needs; and 3) the assigned tasks must be coordinated with hospital management in order to address medical direction needs for the hospital (CMS, 2004).

It is also important, under the commercial reasonableness standard, to continue to evaluate the need for various financial arrangements. By way of example, it may have been commercially reasonable to establish a compensation arrangement with a referring physician to assist with the development of a hospital's electronic medical record. However, after the electronic medical record has been established and is operating satisfactorily, continuing the paid administrative position with the referring physician may not be commercially reasonable.

Likewise, it may have been commercially reasonable at one time to establish a paid stipend arrangement with a hospital-based practice, like a radiology group, but such a stipend will need to be evaluated over time to ensure that it remains commercially reasonable. The hospital must continue to evaluate the need for the stipend in order for the radiology group to provide the number of radiologists deemed necessary by the hospital and for the radiology group to pay its radiologists fair market value compensation. A response such as "we have always paid a stipend" or "we have always done it this way" may not support the commercial reasonableness of the practice.

Why Are Fair Market Value and Commercial Reasonableness Important?

Healthcare entities are mandated by the government to have fair market value and commercially reasonable financial arrangements with referral sources. If the Stark Law applies and the financial arrangement is neither fair market value nor commercially reasonable, then the financial arrangement will not meet an applicable exception where fair market value is required (i.e., rental of office space and equipment, personal service arrangements, employment, isolated transactions, and fair market value). Likewise, a safe harbor under the Anti-Kickback Statute will not be met if the financial arrangement was neither fair market value nor commercially reasonable.

Under the Anti-Kickback Statute, if the compensation arrangement is above fair market value or not commercially reasonable, the government may allege that the excess compensation above fair market value or the arrangement that was not commercially reasonable was provided to the referral source with the intent to induce referrals. Simply stated, excess compensation can be deemed by the government to be intended to induce referrals. At a minimum, compensation above fair market value may be used by the government or a *qui tam* litigant as an indicator of intent. Fair market value supporting documentation can be used to negate this inference.

If the government can prove that the parties intended to establish a compensation arrangement that was neither fair market value nor commercially reasonable, in addition to the violations of the Stark Law and Anti-Kickback Statute, the government can also bring charges under the False Claims Act (FCA), which can triple the damages and impose fines of up to $11,500 per claim or request for payment submitted. This means that for every dollar received by your client from a referral source that was paid excess compensation, the government can seek three times that amount as a penalty under the FCA plus up to $11,500.

Because of this potential liability, you should assist your organization in establishing a process to evaluate all compensation arrangements with referral sources to ensure that they are both fair market value and commercially reasonable.

Approval of Compensation Arrangements

Compliance officers should not be solely responsible for approval of compensation arrangements with referral sources. In typical healthcare organizations, compensation arrangements are commonly developed at the specific business/service line level. By way of example, a service line leader can determine that the orthopedic service line needs an orthopedic surgeon to be a medical director. The service line leader can develop a job description and substantiate a need for the position. The finance department will assist the service line leader in the development of the compensation terms and in budgeting the necessary financial resources to pay for the medical director position. A preferred process is for the commercial reasonableness of the position and fair market value justification for the financial terms to be presented to and approved by a committee responsible for the oversight of the position. The committee can be populated by various operational personnel (e.g., CEO, COO, CFO, legal counsel, chief compliance officer, vice president of human relations, chief medical officer), who should evaluate the fair market value and commercial reasonableness documentation to support the position. The compliance officer should either be a voting member of the committee or participate in the committee's deliberations as an advisor to ensure that sufficient consideration is given to the fair market value and commercial reasonableness documentation. As discussed later in this chapter, the documentation used to substantiate the financial terms should be considered by the committee. The committee should also review any information that explains how and why it was determined that the position is necessary from a business or medical perspective.

A formalized process, such as the use of a committee to approve of financial arrangements with referral sources, shows that the organization recognizes the risks involved in financial arrangements with referral sources and is willing to contribute sufficient resources in the formation and approval process. Without a formalized approval process, various individuals within an organization could attempt to establish financial arrangements with referral sources without strict adherence to legal and regulatory guidelines, including the requirements under the Stark Law and Anti-Kickback Statute. Inconsistent outcomes, including conflicting application of benchmark data, can occur.

If your organization uses an approval committee, minutes of the meeting should be maintained, including a brief summary of the deliberations of the committee related to the factors considered when evaluating whether the compensation arrangement is fair market value and commercially reasonable.

Monitoring of Compensation Arrangements

Assuming that you have documented that the financial arrangement is both fair market value and commercially reasonable, you will next have to continuously monitor the financial arrangement to ensure that it *remains* both fair market value and commercially reasonable during the term of the arrangement. For larger organizations, this is not an easy task.

Financial arrangements may be both fair market value and commercially reasonable at the commencement of the arrangement but fall outside of such standards if they are not monitored. Therefore, as the compliance officer, it is your responsibility to either monitor, or establish a process for monitoring, financial arrangements to ensure that they remain both fair market value and commercially reasonable.

Some examples of financial arrangements that fall out of compliance due to a lack of monitoring include the following:

- Paying a medical director inconsistent with the terms of the contract
- Providing a physician free space or free use of equipment or services not covered by the contract
- Failing to collect lease payments owed by a physician
- Failing to charge a physician increases in rental payments that are required by the contract
- Paying a physician for more hours than stated in the contract
- Providing travel reimbursement for a medical director not covered by the contract
- Continuing to pay a physician after termination or expiration of the contract
- Calculating incentive compensation inconsistent with the contractual terms (e.g., including work relative value units [wRVUs] for services performed by an advanced practice practitioner when compensation should be limited to personally performed services of the compensated physician)

As the compliance officer, you will need to work with the various departments of your organization to ensure that all departments impacted by the financial arrangement know the terms and conditions of the arrangement and will oversee the arrangement consistent with such terms and conditions. By way of example, the person responsible for the oversight of a hospital's real estate department needs to ensure that all physician tenants pay on a timely basis and that any annual increases required by the lease agreement are passed through and paid for by the physician tenants. Service line leaders should ensure that compensated administrative services are performed consistent with the terms of the compensation paid.

You should also educate responsible parties so that they understand their responsibility to ensure that the financial arrangements they oversee are monitored effectively. Training and dedicating monitoring resources are key to effective compliance of compensation arrangements with referral sources.

Approaches to Documenting Fair Market Value

The approach to documenting fair market value and commercially reasonable financial arrangements will depend upon the type of financial arrangement with which you are dealing. There are three types of financial arrangements: *compensation arrangements, business valuations,* and *real estate transactions.* Your approach to documenting the fair market value and commercial reasonableness of each financial arrangement will depend on which type of arrangement you are working with.

Compensation arrangements

As noted above, there is no uniformly recognized standard or body of law regarding how to document compensation arrangements as fair market value. Therefore, you will need to establish a methodology that you believe can be defended if the compensation arrangement is ever challenged.

One option is to hire an independent third party to render an opinion. However, the mere existence of a valuation by an independent third party does not necessarily mean that the valuated compensation is either representative of fair market value or commercially reasonable. By way of example, although Tuomey Healthcare received a third-party valuation of 19 part-time employment arrangements, the United States District Court in South Carolina believed that the compensation arrangements were not fair market value (CMS, 2007). Therefore, if you receive a third-party valuation, either you or an experienced healthcare attorney should review the valuation to assess whether the valuation is sufficiently documented and defensible if questioned.

In the Stark Law Phase II regulations, the Centers for Medicare & Medicaid Services (CMS) established a fair market value safe harbor. Even though the safe harbor was deleted in the Stark Law Phase III regulations, CMS stated that the Phase II fair market safe harbor is still a "prudent methodology." The fair market value safe harbor stated that the hourly compensation would be deemed to be fair market value if the compensation were equal to or less than the average hourly compensation at the 50th percentile from at least four national benchmark surveys, which at that time were as follows:

- Physician Compensation and Productivity Survey (Sullivan, Cotter & Associates, Inc.)
- Physician's Compensation Survey (Hay Group)
- Physician Salary Survey Report (Hospital and Health Care Compensation Services)
- Physician Compensation and Productivity Survey (Medical Group Management Association)
- Hospital and Health Care Compensation Report (ECS Watson Wyatt)
- Integrated Health Networks Compensation Survey (William M. Mercer)

To determine the hourly rates from the annual cash compensation from the benchmark sources, the safe harbor divided the 50th percentile annual cash compensation by 2,000 hours.

Part of the rationale for deleting the Phase II fair market value safe harbor was the concern that if compensation was paid above the 50th percentile, such compensation could be perceived not to be fair market value. The regulation was never intended as a maximum amount for fair market value. Obviously, there are circumstances where physicians should be paid above the 50th percentile. There are even circumstances where physicians should be compensated above the 90th percentile.

As noted in the Phase III Stark Law regulations, using national benchmark sources to document whether a proposed compensation arrangement is fair market value is a prudent process. You can use the Phase II fair market value safe harbor guidance by averaging benchmark sources, which removes some of the disparities between those sources. Alternatively, your organization can use a single benchmark source. However, once your organization establishes a benchmark guideline, unless unique circumstances exist, that guideline should be used as the standard for all of your organization's compensation arrangements.

The benchmark sources will report several compensation and productivity factors by percentile. By way of example, assume that the benchmark source you are using benchmarks annual cash compensation for a particular specialty, as shown in Table 6.1.

TABLE 6.1

Specialty Compensation Benchmark

25th percentile	50th percentile	75th percentile	90th percentile
$100,000	$150,000	$200,000	$275,000

Assuming that your organization wanted to employ a physician on a full-time basis whose specialty is benchmarked by this table, you will need to review several factors to determine where this physician should be plotted against the benchmark data. The easiest way to use the benchmark data is to determine the physician's historical or projected productivity. This can either be in the form of wRVUs, collections for personally performed services, or charges for personally performed services. Assuming that your organization has historical documentation that this physician generates wRVUs for personally performed services at approximately the 75th percentile, then it may be reasonable and defensible to pay the physician approximately $200,000.

In addition to productivity, other subjective factors may be used in to benchmark the physician's compensation. Such subjective factors may include the physician's regional or national reputation, number of books or articles published, number of presentations given, historical compensation, or experience, as well as whether your market is experiencing a deficit in the physician's specialty. The objective is to ensure that sufficient documentation exists, possibly using benchmark data, to defend the compensation arrangement if it is challenged.

The checklist in Table 6.2 can be a guideline for subjective compensation factors.

TABLE 6.2	
Checklist for Fair Market Value Analysis	
Item/Indicator	**Description of Information/Documentation Needed for Fair Market Value Analysis**
1	Curriculum Vitae
2	Bona fide counteroffers
3	Attempts to recruit physicians in a particular specialty without success
4	Documented deficiency of the specialty in the market (e.g., the service area needs four physicians of a particular specialty, but only two physicians of such specialty are currently practicing in the services area)
5	Board certification (or multiple board certifications)
6	National or regional expert in specialty
7	More than 10 years of experience
8	Existence of a documented competing officer
9	Author of publications in specialty
10	Speaking engagements in specialty
11	Documented historical compensation
12	Higher than normal hours worked (more than 2,100 hours)
13	Disproportionate amount of call coverage (more than one out of three days)
14	Need for a certain number of physicians in a specialty with service area not having enough residents/patients (e.g., need to employ one cardiothoracic surgeon, but the service area does not have enough population to keep a single surgeon fully busy)
15	Threats by physician to leave the hospital's service area
16	Only alternative available to the hospital is to use the services of a locum tenens physician at a higher cost (this is known as "but for" paying the physician a particular amount, the only alternative for the hospital is to pay more per hour for a locum tenens physician)
17	Employing a physician because of new technology or new/expanded service line
18	Historic service in a leadership position
19	Does/will physician supervise nonphysician practitioners

This checklist is also included on the downloads page for this book.

Even though using national benchmark data is a "prudent methodology," other methodologies can be used to document financial arrangements as being fair market value. The subjective factors noted earlier can also be used to evaluate financial arrangements from a fair market value perspective. By way of example, if the market has a deficit in a particular specialty and the physician's wRVUs are only at the 25th percentile, it may be reasonable and defensible to compensate the physician at the 75th percentile due to the documented deficit in the specialty. Even though this process references the benchmark data, the compensation may be defensible due to the application of other subjective factors.

Because fair market value and commercial reasonableness is a legally driven definition under both the Stark Law and Anti-Kickback Statute, it is important that you consult with an experienced healthcare attorney when adopting a compensation methodology. It is also important that your organization establish an approval process so that each compensation arrangement can be appropriately vetted, including a review of the documentation to be relied upon, prior to entering into each compensation arrangement.

It is also important to recognize whether the proposed compensation arrangement is an *independent contractor* arrangement as opposed to an *employment* arrangement. Most of the benchmark data benchmarks annual cash compensation for employment arrangements. Thus, when evaluating an independent contractor arrangement, it is possible to add to the benchmark data recognizing that an independent contractor will need to pay for administrative costs and expenses, including benefits and malpractice insurance, in order to provide his or her services.

Call coverage arrangements, like unrestricted call for a specialty through the hospital's emergency department, also create unique challenges for compliance officers. Although benchmark data does exist related to call coverage arrangements, you will need to evaluate the need for compensated call in order to ensure that the call coverage compensation is commercially reasonable. Other factors to consider include the frequency with which a particular specialty is called to provide direct patient care services through the emergency department, and the need for compensated call in your particular market.

Business valuations

Benchmark data does not exist for business valuations. As noted earlier, though, a formal body of knowledge and professional standards governing the appraisal practice for business valuations does exist.

Therefore, if a physician's practice is going to be acquired, the best practice is to engage the services of a business valuation firm that has experience in the healthcare industry. As recommended above, it is important to review the business valuation from a legal perspective to assess whether such valuation is likely to be defensible if ever challenged.

In a business valuation, it is important that *all information* regarding the physician's practice, or other business transaction, be provided to the valuation firm. The valuation firm can generate a defensible valuation only if all information is provided and considered as part of the valuation process.

As discussed earlier in connection with the definition of commercial reasonableness, you will also need to consider whether the acquisition of the physician's practice, or other business transaction, is commercially reasonable for your organization. This will mean that you will need to determine that there is a legitimate business need to acquire the physician's practice.

Real estate valuations

Real estate is a special compliance issue. Because real estate is not a healthcare provider's primary business, healthcare providers, like hospitals, often do not have a full appreciation of the compliance risks involved with the management and leasing of real estate to referral sources. There have been several cases and settlements where real estate was a component of the compliance concern. Therefore, as the compliance officer, you should ensure that your organization has sufficient resources and experience to manage your real estate transactions.

Like business valuations, a formal body of knowledge and professional standards governs the appraisal practice for real estate. A "best practice" is to engage the services of a certified real estate valuation firm that has experience in the healthcare industry. At least once every two to three years, you should seek a valuation of your real estate to determine its market rates. A defensible real estate valuation is one that provides market comparables and a value that is specific to your medical office building. Most frequently, the valuation report will provide a range.

Gross rental vs. triple net rental

It is important to understand whether the valuation range is for gross rental charges, meaning that the rental rate charged is the only amount the physician tenant will pay, or is a triple net rental rate, meaning that the physician will pay a base rental rate and then pay an additional amount based upon the landlord's cost for common area maintenance, which includes utilities, insurance, taxes, and general building maintenance, such as mowing and snow plowing. The real estate valuation firm should also establish a "fair market" for tenant improvements, such as painting and wallpapering or finishing the interior space if it is a new medical office building. The tenant improvements will need to be factored into the overall arrangement from a fair market value perspective.

After you have received a valuation that is specific to your medical office building, then the space leased to referring physicians should be leased at rates consistent with the valuation report.

Time share leases

Time share lease arrangements also represent a special compliance issue for compliance officers. Time share arrangements are arrangements where a physician will rent space on a periodic or sporadic basis (e.g., Monday morning each week). Time share leasing arrangements must be carefully constructed to ensure that the time share tenant is paying an appropriate and fair market value rate for all of the services used by the physician. In order to meet the Stark Law exception for rental of office space, the time share tenant must be the exclusive user of the space when the physician is leasing it on a time shared basis. All of the costs and expenses related to the space must be determined, including the fair value of the office and medical equipment and supplies, when determining the rental charge. Further, if the space is projected to be vacant part of the time, a vacancy factor may need to be applied.

As with any compensation arrangement, it is important to monitor real estate rental arrangements to ensure that the arrangements stay consistent with the terms of the contract. By way of example, if a physician group is leasing Suite 1 but is also occupying Suite 2 because Suite 2 is vacant, such an arrangement would be noncompliant because the physician group is not paying to lease Suite 2.

Another example of monitoring in a time share arrangement would be to ensure that the leasing physician is using the time share suite only during the times listed in the contract. By way of example, if the time share leasing physician is contracted to use the time shared space each Monday morning from 8:00 a.m. until noon, it would be noncompliant for the physician to use the time shared space from 8:00 a.m. until 1:00 p.m. each Monday.

Likewise, if the time share tenant has not leased special medical equipment or personnel from the hospital, the tenant should not use special medical equipment or personnel unless such use is subject to a contract signed by both parties with compensation at fair market value.

Settlements Involving Fair Market Value/Commercial Reasonableness

Several recent settlements have involved allegations that compensation terms involving referral sources, including physicians, were not representative of fair market value and were not commercially reasonable. It is important to note that the settlements described in Table 6.3 contained many allegations and defenses related to fair market value/commercial reasonableness standards. Therefore, even though the issue involved in each settlement does not represent an adjudicated position regarding fair market value/commercial reasonableness, the settlements can be illustrative of the issues being litigated and the challenges involved in complying with the standards of fair market value and commercial reasonableness. As you can see in Table 6.3, many compensation arrangements and many types of providers were involved in recent settlements. Therefore, no provider or compensation type is immune to fair market value challenges.

TABLE 6.3

Date	Entity	Amount	Issue
November 15, 2019	Sutter Medical Center	$30,500,000	Hospital leased physician assistant services from physician group with group billing, retaining reimbursement, and above fair market value for medical director and call services.
September 3, 2019	Grant Memorial Hospital	$661,386.57	Paid bonus payments to physicians that were not consistent with the terms of employment agreements and not reflective of fair market value for OB/GYN services.
September 3, 2019	Oxford Immunotec, Inc.	$88,780.74	Collection, processing, and handling payments paid to physicians and physician groups inconsistent with Stark Law and Anti-Kickback Statute requirements.
April 4, 2019	Great River Health System, Inc.	$3,008,326.50	Alleged excessive compensation inconsistent with fair market value.
February 19, 2019	Union Hospital of Cecil County, Inc.	$457,213.07	Provision of free support services inconsistent with fair market value to physicians.
December 31, 2018	Gastroenterology Associates of Piedmont, P.A.	$188,900.89	Remuneration provided to two anesthesia practices in form of below-market rent and free anesthesia-related drugs and supplies.

TABLE 6.3 (CONT.)			
Date	**Entity**	**Amount**	**Issue**
December 18, 2018	Cancer Treatment Centers of America Global, Inc. (and affiliated entities)	$8,220,814.50	Remuneration provided to physicians inconsistent with services and fair market value in exchange for referrals.
October 24, 2018	Presence Care Transformation Corporation, Presence Chicago Hospitals Network, and Presence Central and Suburban Hospitals Networks	$461,130.66	Above fair market value compensation for electroencephalography and electromyography interpretation services and medical director services.
October 23, 2018	St. Francis Health, LLC	$3,273,181	Incentive payments for performance of metrics that were not met by compensated physicians.
September 24, 2018	Rex Hospital, Inc. d/b/a UNC Rex Healthcare	$2,277,762	Physician was paid salary and bonus in excess of compensation paid for physician's services by a hospital with which Rex had an employee lease arrangement.
August 30, 2018	San Juan Regional Medical Center, Inc.	$50,000	Above fair market value paid to a physician for land that was leased as a ground lease.
August 6, 2018	Wahiawa Hospital Association and Wahiawa General Hospital	$100,000	Hospital paid below market for leasing of office space.
May 15, 2018	Visionworks of America, Inc.	$3,668,961	Below fair market value office and equipment leases and failure to collect rental amounts under space and equipment leases.
May 15, 2018	Cheyenne Regional Medical Center	$2,099,462.30	Compensation paid to physicians that was greater than fair market value and allegedly for costs that should have been borne by physician practice.
April 24, 2018	Heartford Hospital	$423,017.45	Rent at less than fair market value for office space.
February 9, 2018	CHRISTUS Health	$148,095	Above fair market value compensation for medical distributorship owned by referring physician.
January 5, 2018	St. Agnes Healthcare, Inc.	$2,231,722.50	Above fair market value compensation and improper administrative payments.
February 22, 2017	Cavalier County Memorial Hospital Association	$750,000	Above fair market value compensation to two physicians and a nurse practitioner.
October 26, 2017	St. Vincent Frankfort Hospital, Inc.	$120,066.17	Below fair market value rental rate.
March 17, 2017	Crittenton Hospital Medical Center and Crittenton Cancer Center	$3,274,153.90	Above fair market value compensation paid to physicians.
February 8, 2017	Metro Health Corporation	$2,305,743.39	Above fair market value compensation to two independent contractor physician groups for neurosurgical and general surgery services.

Source: Information obtained from original source as well as Provider Self-Disclosure Settlements from the Office of Inspector General found at https://oig.hhs.gov/fraud/enforcement/cmp/psds.asp.

Conclusion

Documenting and monitoring financial arrangements between referral sources is a pinnacle issue for compliance officers. Many of the large settlements and cases involve financial arrangements that are alleged to be either not fair market value or not commercially reasonable. Therefore, the best practice is for the compliance officer to establish guidelines and policies and procedures regarding how the organization is to document fair market value and commercial reasonableness for all financial arrangements with referral sources, including physicians, and a structured approval process for each such financial arrangement. The structured approval process should involve individuals who are not directly involved with the negotiation of the subject financial arrangement.

Even though fair market value and commercial reasonableness can seem challenging, through collaboration within your organization as well as the assistance of outside attorneys and consultants, this aspect of your compliance program can be appropriately managed.

References

Centers for Medicare & Medicaid Services (CMS). (2004). Medicare Program; Physicians' referrals to health care entities with which they have financial relationships (Phase II). *Federal Register.* www.federalregister.gov/documents/2004/03/26/04-6668/medicare-program-physicians-referrals-to-health-care-entities-with-which-they-have-financial

CMS. (2007). Medicare Program; Physicians' referrals to health care entities with which they have financial relationships (Phase III). *Federal Register.* www.federalregister.gov/documents/2007/09/05/07-4252/medicare-program-physicians-referrals-to-health-care-entities-with-which-they-have-financial

United States of America (U.S.) ex. rel., *Darryl L. Kaczmarczyk, et. al, v. SCCI Hospital Ventures, Inc.* d/b/a SCCI Hospital Houston Central, U.S. District Court, Southern District of Texas, Houston, Division, No. H-99-1031, July 14, 2004.

U.S. ex rel. *Drakeford v. Tuomey Healthcare System*, 2013 WL 5503695 (DSC 2013).

Chapter 7
Internal Strategies for Best Practices

As a compliance officer, you should be seeking to establish best practices regarding compliance risk areas. Once a risk area is identified, either because an issue was discovered or the risk area has become a focus of the government, you should establish internal safeguards and protocols to minimize risks.

These internal strategies should involve all stakeholders that have responsibility for or oversight regarding the risk area.

This chapter is intended to identify and discuss risk areas on which healthcare compliance officers should focus that are not otherwise covered by a separate chapter in this book. This chapter is not intended to identify best practices for all risk areas, as each organization is unique and each industry sector has its own risk areas that are not generally applicable to all healthcare industry sectors.

This chapter also discusses best practices for structuring the compliance function. Structure and operational accountability will depend greatly on the size and financial health of the organization and the organization's culture. Although this chapter will outline some guidelines related to structural best practices, these guidelines should be viewed as suggestions.

Quality-of-Care Issues

One risk area is quality of care. This issue is a top priority for the U.S. Department of Health and Human Services (HHS), Centers for Medicare & Medicaid Services (CMS), the HHS Office of Inspector General (OIG), and the U.S. Department of Justice (DOJ). It also has always been an issue for state surveyors, state attorneys general, and Medicaid Fraud Control Units as they examine skilled nursing facilities, hospitals, and other medical providers. In fact, quality of care is a regular topic on the OIG's *Work Plan*.

Because quality of care continues to be a priority for both the state and federal government, consider the following questions and concerns when examining your compliance program:

- Evaluate the procedure in place to monitor quality of care. Is an oversight board in place? Is quality of care part of your compliance plan? How are quality-of-care problems handled?
- Educate staff members, both professional and nonprofessional, on quality of care and the ethical responsibility each has in this area. Is quality of care in your mission statement? Are the goals and charitable duties of the facility in concert with quality of care?
- Immediately address problems or concerns regarding quality of care and errors. Is there a clear line of communication among the staff, the compliance officer, and the board to address

quality-of-care issues? Are inquiries and questions handled discreetly and in confidence? Are inquiry results made available to the complainant and others in a timely manner? Are quality concerns appropriately addressed with the patient?

- Conduct internal audits and evaluations to ensure quality of care in all areas of the facility. Monitor patient complaints and satisfaction surveys to determine whether quality issues are being reported.
- Assess malpractice lawsuits to determine whether systemic quality issues may exist.
- Accreditation reviews can highlight potential quality issues, especially if citations are noted.
- Use quality of care to your advantage. Recognize and promote the organization's effectiveness and efficiency to the government and, more importantly, to the public. Quality of care, correction of errors, and the promotion of good delivery systems will drive down the cost of malpractice insurance and give beneficiaries the services and care they need.

Are Quality-of-Care Issues Compliance Issues?
Federal prosecutors and law enforcement officers view as false claims those claims submitted by healthcare facilities when a patient has been harmed or injured as a result of the treatment and those claims submitted for substantially substandard care. Enforcers use the False Claims Act to prosecute those cases. In other words, the government will not pay for healthcare that does not meet the minimum level of quality (e.g., a facility performs a service so poorly that the service was essentially worthless). The government intends to reimburse for services that provide necessary treatment or stabilization according to specialty standards. When the treatment provided and billed does not meet this standard, the government views such claims for reimbursement as false claims.

Compliance Leaders and Quality of Care

Compliance officers play a key role in addressing quality of care in America's hospitals. Your job is to identify and address risks facing your organization and to take care of your most important stakeholders—your patients—by ensuring that they receive the best possible care.

Insufficient quality can violate the Medicare *Conditions of Participation* and professional and facility licensing statutes. It can also put your organization at risk for tort and False Claims Act (FCA) liability.

Many compliance officers already oversee quality-of-care issues. Compliance officers who have implemented best practices use the following strategies to safeguard quality of care:

1. Assign staff members overlapping responsibilities in compliance and quality of care. For example, many members of a hospital's compliance committee also serve on the quality committee. Members of both committees should focus on quality-of-care issues as part of their monitoring system.
2. Involve physicians. Find several well-respected physicians who will work with you to get other physicians involved in improving quality of care. Involve your CEO and board in this process.

3. Make sure that your policies and procedures actually work. Consider appointing a compliance liaison in each department or service line to make sure that your organization's compliance and oversight hierarchy includes the rank-and-file healthcare leaders. When making decisions that affect compliance and quality, integrate the organization's leaders into the process.
4. Analyze how new systems will affect medical and billing errors. For example, although an electronic order processing system will likely improve efficiency, errors may increase as you implement the system. Test the system after implementation to ensure compliant outcomes. Analyze every process change to determine how the change may increase risk for the institution, providers, and patients.
5. Consider public opinion when you decide how much to emphasize ensuring quality of care, and realize that quality-of-care problems can be more detrimental to your organization than billing errors. For example, when the DOJ announced that it was investigating two Tenet Healthcare physicians, the value of the entity's stock fell 26%. Quality-of-care issues will put you on the front page of the newspaper and may result in a loss of trust and business.
6. Implement an adverse event–reporting system. Look at the issues being reported to identify and assess quality concerns and to analyze what process or procedure caused the issue. You will also need to make sure that employees are using the adverse event–reporting system. If they are not, it may be an indication that they fear retaliation for reporting quality or compliance concerns.
7. Address quality management from a clinical standpoint. The Joint Commission recommends having in place a planned, systematic, organizationwide approach to performance management and improvement.
8. Analyze quality indicators as reported from time to time by CMS or other payer or quality oversight organizations. One quality indicator is to give patients who arrive with heart attacks aspirin or beta-blockers immediately. Test these quality indicators in your facility to determine how your organization compares.
9. Work with your quality committee to develop clinical guidelines. Note that some physicians may see such guidelines as a way to standardize medicine, which they may not like because they want to use their clinical judgment and perhaps don't want to follow standardized guidelines. Nevertheless, it's becoming more common for the standard of care to be well defined. The involvement of your medical staff in the development and implementation of the clinical guidelines are extremely important.
10. Establish priorities based on how your data compare to benchmarks. For clinical indicators, monitor your performance against your organizational goals and compare your results to those of facilities similar in size or geographic region. Get a sense of what the outcomes are and whether the indicators are within normal limits. Look at InterQual (*www.interqual.com*) for protocols and data.
11. Make sure that your quality committee meets regularly. Establish priorities, choose what you're going to monitor, and then get the data. Be sure to follow up with outlier physicians if you identify any problems or trends.

12. Conduct an internal review of supporting documentation for procedures your organization is focusing on for quality improvement. Such documentation could include the charge ticket, medical record, discharge summary, and bill submitted for reimbursement. Compare the procedures that took place to what was actually billed. As part of your review, you should assess the outcome of the procedures or services performed and compare with expected outcomes. If your organization's outcomes are below expectation based upon the acuity of the patients reviewed, the procedure or service may be added to the list of items targeted for quality improvement. This review may also provide insight as to whether correct billing codes were used.
13. Reengineer your peer review process. Peer review by medical staff is the accepted basic process for ensuring quality, but it's not geared to detect unnecessary services. Most peer review occurs only after bad outcomes. Therefore, build in a random and routine examination of procedures.
14. Pay close attention to indications of quality problems. If you get a complaint from a nurse, physician, or patient, look into it rather than simply filing it away. Be sure to follow up on it. In your record of the problem, include the allegation and what you did to address the problem.
15. Review denials and readmissions. Doing so could help bridge the gap between utilization review and compliance, because the two departments help prevent problems and errors. An investigation will indicate which physicians are experiencing high readmissions and denials so you can determine whether there is a pattern or trend that needs to be addressed.
16. Report substantiated allegations of substandard care to the compliance and quality committees and, if systemic quality issues are identified, to the hospital board.
17. Consider hiring independent outside experts to assist your organization in assessing quality matters.
18. Monitor websites that report quality outcomes for your organization (e.g., *leapfroggroup.org*). If negative quality issues are reported, such issues should be a target for improvement. Likewise, if you believe that a quality reporting organization is reporting issues that are not valid, contact the organization to determine whether additional information can be provided in order to improve the quality rating.
19. Train your physicians and other providers regarding the importance of documenting comorbidities. Failure to document all comorbidities being experienced by a patient may significantly impact your organization's quality rankings. By way of example, if your organization has a higher-than-average morbidity rate for a particular disease state, it may be because your organization serves a patient population that has a higher frequency of comorbidities than the population served by other providers. Accurately documenting comorbidities is not just about increased revenue; it is also necessary to ensure that your organization is ranked appropriately on quality indicators.

How Compliance Officers Can Help Mend the Quality Crisis

Although you don't directly treat patients, you can do a lot to improve their care. As the compliance officer, you should do the following to safeguard quality of care in your organization:

- Ensure compliance with state law and Joint Commission requirements for external reporting of adverse events.
- Either attend meetings or review meeting minutes of quality oversight committees.
- Meet periodically with the organization's quality officer.
- Investigate allegations of falsified medical records related to patient care.
- Learn the Joint Commission patient safety requirements. See *www.jointcommission.org* for details.
- Regularly obtain reports within your institution on specific patient safety projects.
- Ensure that an internal reporting system exists for adverse events, their causes, and efforts to prevent recurrence. Review these adverse events and the corrective actions implemented, and then make sure that appropriate monitoring mechanisms are in place to decrease the likelihood of the adverse event occurring in the future.
- Become familiar with system requirements to ensure patient safety, and raise the issue of patient safety implications of new technology.
- Ensure that patient safety issues are regularly placed on the agendas of the board and executive committee meetings.
- Include physicians, nurses, and other professional personnel in safety and quality decisions and oversight.
- Investigate patient and family concerns related to safety and quality.
- Communicate your institution's commitment to quality improvement and avoiding errors as part of your compliance communications.
- If lack of resources or training is the cause of quality issues, advocate for increased resources and training in order to minimize quality problems.
- In order to address quality issues, a best practice would be to have at least one registered nurse and at least one physician on your compliance committee.
- Monitor the adverse reporting process, root cause analysis process, and corrective actions to ensure that quality issues are being investigated and corrected.

Patient care trouble areas

Because patient complaints can increase your facility's risk of being subject to an investigation, your organization must follow up on any quality-of-care concerns. Here we will discuss six hot spots in which providers often run into quality-of-care trouble.

Adverse events

Adverse events can lead to investigations—especially when they receive publicity. Fire, deaths, and complaints filed outside the organization (e.g., with regulators such as your state department of health) can draw investigators to your facility.

For example, a patient from a long-term care facility may be admitted to a hospital, and the emergency room staff there may find that the patient is in such poor condition due to significant and untreated bed sores that the hospital is required to report the long-term care facility to the state.

Noncompliant research

Inappropriate or noncompliant research activity draws attention—these days, mistakes do not have to be egregious to gain notice. Therefore, it is extremely important to have a well-developed auditing and monitoring plan of all research being conducted in your facility. Review research protocols and test the research activities to ensure that the research is being conducted consistent with the established protocols.

Keep track of all types of research at your facility, and ensure that quality control policies are in place. This is essential especially for the patients who are participants in clinical research studies. You will need to make sure that prior to participating in a research study, patients know and understand the risks and benefits, including alternatives, and provide informed consent. If regulators come in and ask you questions about ongoing research, you must be well informed in your answers. Further, billing issues related to patients participating in clinical trials should be monitored for compliance.

Problematic documentation

Preventing problematic or deficient documentation is an age-old challenge in healthcare and can be extremely frustrating for everyone, including compliance officers and auditors.

Accurate medical record documentation should reflect the condition of the patient, any comorbidities, the services and procedures performed, and the quality of care your facility provided.

If you can't prove that you provided the required standard of care because the medical record documentation is deficient and a claim is submitted, the claim may be a false claim and be subject to FCA liability. You also could be subject to other noncompliance violations because you could not prove that you provided the standard of care you agreed to provide in a contractual relationship.

A failure to properly credential hospital staff members also contributes to improper documentation. Medicare considers claims for services provided by unqualified or noncredentialed personnel to be false claims.

For example, one provider hired a physical therapist (PT) and conducted the appropriate background checks. Everything checked out fine, but the individual wound up on the Medicare exclusion list later that year. The facility missed the update because it performed background checks only for new hires. By the time the discovery was made, the facility had already erroneously submitted claims for services by that PT.

Therefore, although the facility put forth all the correct documentation to demonstrate that the individual had provided the care required from the time he was hired, the organization was still required to return the money and could face other potential compliance violations because the provider was excluded by Medicare.

The use of electronic medical records has also created compliance and quality concerns. Although electronic medical records can allow for more efficient documentation of services provided compared with paper medical records, providers must know and understand the compliance and quality risks associated with electronic medical records. Many electronic medical records provide template documentation for disease states. However, when a provider uses template documentation, he or she should ensure that the documentation is accurate and specific to the patient. Quality concerns can occur if the template does not accurately describe either the medical condition of the patient or the service provided. By way of example, if the template documentation for hypertension includes references to the patient's smoking history but the patient is a nonsmoker, inappropriate documentation will be submitted in the patient's medical record.

Likewise, if the template describes the normal physician examination that a provider would conduct for a particular disease state, the use of the template language would be inappropriate if the provider did not perform all of the physical reviews as contained in the template.

Failure to adhere to safety requirements

Patient safety is at the root of all patient care quality issues, and safety incidents attract the attention of external eyes. The Joint Commission recommends that facilities follow the tracer method to find quality-of-care problems. This method tracks each patient through his or her healthcare experience, verifying that each step is documented.

The Leapfrog Group is one organization that tracks hospital quality efforts. Organizations such as Leapfrog and the Institute of Medicine track certain aspects of healthcare quality, partly in response to the attention that the public and media have devoted to quality-of-care issues.

Failure to follow up with corrective action

A major problem in auditing and monitoring is failing to execute and follow up on a corrective action plan. Many facilities have in place a comprehensive quality improvement process, creating quality-of-care committees and setting plans for performance improvement. But sometimes these committees lack plans to ensure that any weaknesses are addressed. All reasonable allegations should be reviewed, with the appropriate allocation of resources depending on the nature of the allegation and the need for closure or other corrective action. As the compliance officer, you should review the workings of the quality-of-care committees to ensure that they have sufficient resources and are functioning appropriately.

Failure to define quality measures

On the most basic level, providers need to define quality-of-care measurements. This task should not be delegated to a low-level manager; rather, senior management needs to accept responsibility for setting the organization's standards. However, if you decide to set a higher bar for a standard of care in a particular area, then enforcers will hold you to that standard. Ensure that you meet that standard so others won't find your organization deficient.

Corporate Compliance for Board Members

Corporate directors shoulder more responsibility for their organization's regulatory compliance than ever before. Although corporate compliance cannot occur without everyone's participation, the job of ensuring that an effective compliance program exists falls on the governing board and upper management.

Members of the governing board are responsible for knowing the content and operation of your organization's compliance and ethics program in order to provide effective oversight. The Sarbanes-Oxley Act, the U.S. Sentencing Guidelines, the OIG compliance guidance, state legislation, and court cases offer rules, regulations, prohibitions, and suggested best practices for corporate compliance and board oversight.

Directors of healthcare organizations have important corporate compliance responsibilities. Healthcare organizations must meet myriad requirements governing the provision and reimbursement of medical services, and noncompliance could result in requirements to repay funds to the government, government audits, corporate integrity agreements, significant penalties, and negative publicity. In egregious cases, criminal liability may be imposed. The responsibility for compliance failure ultimately rests on the shoulders of leadership—especially the governing board and upper management. The board and upper management must ensure that sufficient resources are dedicated to the compliance program and that the compliance officer has sufficient power and authority in the organization to effectuate change if noncompliant issues are discovered. This requires the compliance officer to make regular reports to the board or a committee of the board.

Inaction may become a basis for liability, as the government and shareholders could potentially seek to hold board members accountable for failing to monitor compliance programs effectively. The landmark 1996 Caremark case stands for the proposition that, in theory, the failure to monitor an organization's compliance program could become a basis for board liability. Even a casual perusal of media coverage related to major cases, investigations, and settlements underscores this issue. Board members are frequently identified by media, especially if the organization is a government or tax-exempt entity. This can lead the public to believe that the board members were culpable in the alleged compliance violations regardless of whether this is the case.

It is important to note that most board members of hospital organizations, for example, are not involved in the healthcare industry. Therefore, it is important to educate board members regarding fraud and abuse risks, as such risks are not normal in most industries. As an example, a banker on a hospital board may take a customer out to an expensive dinner to "thank" a client for past bank-related business. In this case, the business dinner is legal. The same banker, however, may not know that if a CFO of the hospital takes a referring physician to an expensive dinner to "thank" the physician for past referrals or as an inducement for future referrals, this is potentially a criminal violation under the Anti-Kickback Statute. What may be legal in normal business to thank a customer (e.g., a bank president and a client) may be illegal in the healthcare industry (e.g., hospital CFO and a referring physician).

Compliance Reporting Process

An organization should have a progressive reporting process. By way of example, employees should report issues to their supervisors, a higher-ranking officer, or the compliance officer or use an anonymous hotline. These reporting avenues should be promoted within the organization. It is important to encourage employees to use any reporting avenue, and a best practice is to promote no single path of communication or chain of command reporting. As an example, requiring an employee to report the issue to their supervisor prior to reporting the issue to the compliance officer (an example of "chain of command reporting") should be discouraged.

Hotline calls

Hotline calls are among the simplest ways for your organization to identify compliance issues. To benefit from your compliance program, seek feedback and have mechanisms in place for finding issues. If an organization has a hotline but fails to monitor it, that defeats the purpose and shows a lack of commitment to compliance.

Encourage the use of your hotline. Promote the use of the hotline in new employee education, in annual compliance training, and through posters, screensavers, and stickers on phones. Emphasize that employees who report issues should not fear retaliation because the compliance program prohibits retaliation for good-faith reports. If your organization does not receive any hotline calls, it does not mean that there are no compliance concerns. Even despite assurances to the contrary, employees may fear retaliation and thus choose not to bring issues to your attention.

Audit your anonymous hotline to make sure that the compliance department investigates calls in a timely and thorough manner. Use your audit to identify whether employees need more education on using the hotline.

Test employee knowledge

Survey staff members to find out whether they know about the hotline and what number to call. Ask them what types of information they may report to the hotline and whether they would consider using it. In addition, ask employees whether they think your organization takes hotline calls seriously. Based upon employee feedback, additional training on or promotion of the hotline may be necessary.

Examine HR-related calls

Either HR or the compliance department should follow up on each call to collect more information and to determine whether there is a serious problem. This is important because some HR issues can involve legal and compliance matters.

Many hotline reports are related to HR concerns, which is fine. If employees are using the hotline to report HR concerns, it means that they understand the hotline to be a method for reporting concerns and that they do not fear retaliation.

Make sure that the HR department handles all HR-related calls. If you keep getting the same types of calls over and over again, either someone isn't paying attention or there is something really wrong that your organization is not effectively addressing. Review the HR log and its follow-up documentation. Contact callers to determine whether HR promptly handled their issues. Track response times to determine an average, and then set a new goal if the average time is too slow. See "Identify problem areas" later in this chapter for details.

Although the compliance department is not the HR department, if an HR issue is reported through the hotline, the compliance officer should oversee the investigation and closure process to make sure that the issue is thoroughly investigated and appropriate action is taken. You should make sure that the HR department understands that your oversight is due to the issue being reported through the anonymous hotline, not that you are taking over an HR function. The HR department should view the compliance department as an advocate, not an adversary.

Even though the HR department may have a separate reporting process for HR issues, the use of the anonymous hotline should not be perceived by the HR department as problematic, given that it shows that the employees do not fear retaliation as a result of its use. As the compliance officer, you should tell employees that if they feel comfortable bringing HR issues directly to the HR department, they should do so; however, add that it's also okay to use the hotline if they are more comfortable with that method.

Sample hotline calls

Choose a sample based on your organization's size, its call volume, and the degree of confidence you want for your audit. If your facility receives few calls, you can review them quickly. If your hotline is very active, use a sample of 25–50 calls. The focus of the review is to make sure that employees are using the hotline, concerns are thoroughly investigated, and appropriate closure is implemented. Depending on the nature of the issue, if the caller identifies himself or herself, closure should be provided to the caller.

Gather documentation

Examine the hotline log and files that document how your organization resolved each issue. Identify the data that compliance staff members capture on the hotline log for each call, and then determine what additional data you will need when you select the sample.

Review the following documentation:

- Forms used to track comments from callers
- Letters received from employees about compliance issues
- Reports used to track and trend calls
- Results of investigations and steps taken to investigate complaints
- Filing and numbering systems
- Procedures for anonymous calls
- Hotline policies and procedures
- Investigative reports
- Whether corrective action is documented
- Closure, if appropriate, with employee reporting concerns

Make sure that your organization documents calls made directly to the compliance department reporting compliance issues or concerns. These calls should be tracked and investigation activity and corrective action documented given that direct calls to the compliance department are part of your program's reporting process.

Review hotline policies

Review your organization's compliance plan and hotline policies. Interview compliance staff members responsible for the hotline, and ask them about their procedures. Determine in advance how you will evaluate and assess how HR and similar complaints are resolved.

Review documentation

Pay attention to the appropriate balance of capturing the salient facts on the call. Limit the documentation to the facts being alleged. Do not document motive or intent, as these will be determined as part of your investigation or review. The documentation should be limited to who did it, what the person did, when it was done, and where it was done. This is to prevent creating a negative conclusion that is not substantiated or confirmed when investigated. Callers will sometimes say inflammatory things without knowing whether they have actually occurred; transcribing these statements exactly may jeopardize the organization if the allegations are overblown. Instead, make sure that documentation fairly represents the complaint and the individual named in it.

Identify problem areas

Make sure that the compliance or HR department investigates and closes calls as soon as possible (usually within 30 days). Ensure that the compliance department resolves the problem or forwards it to the appropriate individual. Ask a sample of callers whether they are satisfied with the process used by the organization to resolve their problem or issue. Be careful here: The focus is on how the organization responded, not necessarily on whether the caller agrees with the outcome. The hotline should be checked regularly so that calls don't languish for days or weeks.

Measure effectiveness

Measure your hotline's effectiveness by examining whether callers share viable compliance issues. Also, consider whether employees are using other practical avenues to report problems, like direct reports speaking to supervisors, the compliance officer, or the compliance department. The number of calls your hotline receives doesn't always indicate its effectiveness. In fact, some providers may not receive many calls to their hotlines if the employees do not fear retaliation and use other direct reporting processes. A better measure of the hotline's effectiveness is to test whether employees understand its purpose.

Review outside contracts

If you use an outside hotline company, make sure that your organization receives the calls in compliance with its contract. You also need to know whether employees are using the hotline for its intended purpose. Call the hotline to ensure that the line is working and that operators answer calls promptly. Ask managers and employees whether they have a problem using the hotline. You will also need to make sure that the hotline company is getting the call information to the correct person, especially if you are part of a multifacility organization.

Monitor calls

Your audit findings will determine how closely you should monitor your hotline. For example, if you find that the compliance or HR department is not retrieving calls in a timely manner, keep an eye on the situation. If managers or other employees are retaliating against hotline callers, monitor future HR actions involving known users of the hotline. Base monitoring on the size of your organization and the risk associated with the problems you identify.

Retaliation

As the compliance officer, you are responsible for protecting from retaliation employees who report compliance concerns in good faith. You should keep a list of all employees who have reported compliance concerns, and if corrective actions are taken against such employees, you should investigate to make sure that such corrective action was not taken, directly or indirectly, as a result of their report. A good way to do so is to provide a list of all employees who have brought a compliance concern to the attention of the organization, either through the hotline or another reporting mechanism, to the HR department. If a corrective action is brought against any employees who are on the list, the HR department should contact you to make sure that the corrective action is not due, in part, to the employee bringing the compliance concern forward. Overt retaliation may be easy to detect. However, covert retaliation can also occur, sometimes disguised as "poor performance." By way of example, an employee could have had stellar performance reviews but receive a substandard performance evaluation after bringing a compliance concern to the attention of the organization.

Whistleblowers

Each year, the government increases the number of *qui tam* cases it pursues. The stakes are high, according to compliance officers—and that's why legal experts suggest that you don't wait until the government is at your doorstep to decide how to handle a whistleblower. *Qui tam* whistleblowers have a financial incentive to bring concerns to the government's attention, as they can receive up to 25% of the government's recovery, depending upon whether the government intervenes in the case. In fact, the authors have noted over the years that most cases are brought by *qui tam* whistleblowers, not through independent action by CMS, the DOJ, or the OIG.

Even though an effective compliance program lowers the risk of a *qui tam* case, organizations that receive more than $5 million per year from the Medicaid program are required to educate employees regarding their right to bring issues to the attention of the government under the FCA. As part of this education, organizations are also required to inform employees that if they do bring issues to the attention of the government, their employer cannot retaliate against them. This education was mandated by the Deficit Reduction Act of 2005.

Preventing whistleblowers: Exit interviews

Interview exiting employees to help ensure that they bring concerns to you rather than immediately becoming whistleblowers. Don't let potential whistleblowers walk out your door without giving them the opportunity to share their compliance concerns.

Although exit interviews are primarily an HR function allowing employees to air their grievances, you're missing out if you don't ask employees to tell you about any known or suspected compliance violations of which they are aware. Use the exit interview questionnaire included on the downloads page for this book as a guide. Any such allegations should be investigated in the same manner as other compliance allegations.

If employees tell you their concerns and believe that they are being taken seriously, they might be less inclined to become whistleblowers. In other words, if you don't give them the opportunity to tell you, they may feel compelled to tell someone else—such as the government. Exit interviews also can alert you to breakdowns in the compliance program, such as employees not knowing how to use the hotline.

During exit interviews, ask the right questions. In addition to covering HR issues, ask employees whether they know about the compliance program, whether compliance information was communicated adequately, and whether the organization is coding, billing, and documenting appropriately. You can also ask whether the departing employee knows of any inappropriate financial arrangements between your organization and a referral source, such as a physician.

Someone from compliance should conduct the interview only if the interview relates primarily to compliance or if it is a follow-up to compliance issues identified in the HR exit interview.

Preventing whistleblowers: Effective reporting process

One of the best ways to prevent potential whistleblowers is to have an effective reporting process in which employees feel comfortable bringing compliance concerns to the organization's attention. In order to do this, employees need to feel that the organization will take their concerns seriously, conduct an effective review or investigation, and implement appropriate corrective action.

Most employees want to do the right thing, and they want to work for an organization that they believe is compliant and ethical. As such, most employees would rather have the organization address compliance concerns than become a whistleblower for the government. Most whistleblowers say that they tried to bring their concerns to the organization's attention and that the organization either did not investigate or did not implement appropriate corrective action. Further, some whistleblowers have stated that they feared retaliation, such as losing their job, so they felt that the only alternative was to bring the complaint to the government as a *qui tam* litigant.

Operating an effective compliance program that encourages the discussion and review of compliance issues decreases the likelihood of facing a challenge by a *qui tam* whistleblower.

Anonymous reports

Set up processes, especially through the hotline, to allow anonymous reports. Treat anonymous reports seriously. Although it is a normal human reaction to contemplate the identity of the anonymous reporter, do not dwell on the reporter's possible identity. Treat the anonymous report with the same sense of urgency as reports where the reporter is known. It has been the author's experience that many serious and high-risk issues are reported anonymously out of fear of retaliation, even if the organization has a strong nonretaliation policy and practice. Focusing on the source and identity of the anonymous reporter could, under certain circumstances, be a form of retaliation. When it comes to anonymous reports, your mantra should be, "It does not matter who it is." The focus should be on *what* was reported, not on *who* filed the report.

Compliance Tracking Log

Another best practice is for the compliance officer to maintain and continuously update a compliance issue tracking log. The compliance issue tracking log is used by the compliance officer and compliance committee to identify each compliance issue reported to the compliance officer or organization, the status of the review/investigation, and the closure of the compliance issue. The compliance tracking log can use any format that fits with the operations and structure of the organization. However, key issues to be placed on the compliance tracking log are as follows:

- Date of compliance report
- Source of compliance report (e.g., hotline, direct report issued to compliance officer, payer inquiry, anonymous, patient)

- Type of compliance issue (e.g., billing/reimbursement, referral source financial arrangement, privacy/security, quality, HR)
- General description of issue being reported
- Risk assigned (high/medium/low)
- Person to whom investigation is assigned
- Status of investigation
- Date of closure

See an example of the format of a compliance tracking log on this book's downloads page.

The compliance officer should assess risks related to the compliance issues being reported. The compliance officer can use a risk assignment like "high," "medium," or "low." High issues could be, by way of example, billing reviews where potential repayments are expected or issues dealing with financial arrangements with referral sources. Medium risks can include issues like privacy/security or HR concerns. Low risks could include requests for education or requests related to information regarding billing, coding, documentation, or reimbursement guidelines.

Maintain a log for open issues and a log for issues that are closed. It is acceptable to track open issues and closed issues on the same database if the database has the ability to generate a list that segregates the open issues from the closed issues.

Another issue to consider is the closure of compliance issues. A best practice could include giving the compliance officer the authority to close all low-risk issues. Medium issues can be recommended to the compliance committee, with authority for the closure of the compliance issue being based upon a vote of the compliance committee. High risks can be closed through the recommendation of the compliance officer or approval by the compliance committee with a recommendation and approval of the closure of the high-risk issue through the board, a board committee, or another executive committee (e.g., the CEO's cabinet/council).

Compliance Structure

The OIG compliance guidance does not mandate the specific structure of the compliance function within an organization. However, the OIG compliance guidance recommends that the compliance officer be a high-ranking officer within the organization. This is so that the compliance officer has the authority necessary to make compliance decisions and recommendations. It is easier for a compliance officer to effectuate change and to address compliance issues if the compliance officer is, for example, an executive vice president as opposed to a midlevel manager. Titles equate to authority. Obviously, the specific title and authority will depend upon the size and scope of the organization.

It is also imperative that the compliance function operate through a committee. The best practice is for the compliance officer to chair the compliance committee. The committee must be populated with officers and executives who can provide compliance oversight and effectuate compliance change within the various operational divisions of the organization. Some recommended members include CFO, COO, chief HR officer, chief legal officer, director of patient financial services, and executives over key operational divisions such as laboratory, nursing, physician practices, information technology, and marketing. It may be appropriate not to include the CEO on the committee; this may allow the CEO to be a "sounding board" or arbitrator for an issue if it cannot be resolved through the compliance committee or the compliance officer.

Compliance officers should use the compliance committee as a working committee to review all open compliance issues and to provide operational guidance on how the compliance function can help resolve issues.

Compliance committee meetings should have an agenda. Best practice agenda items include approval of minutes, review of minutes of other committees that impact compliance (i.e., committee that approves of financial arrangements), review of compliance issue tracking log and approval of items for closure, review of current audit/investigations, review of outstanding monitoring activities, and known governmental/payer reviews/investigations.

If a compliance review/investigation is intended to be covered by the attorney client privilege, the attorney through whom the privilege will be claimed should participate in the portion of the compliance committee during which the issue is addressed. The minutes of the activities of the compliance committee relating to such an issue should be separately maintained by and through legal counsel. Compliance committee members participating in a meeting should be advised when the discussion is intended to be covered by attorney-client privilege and manage their involvement with the understanding of how to protect that privilege. Strict confidentiality regarding the privileged discussions should be maintained.

It's crucial that committee members regularly attend meetings. By actively participating, members emphasize the importance of the compliance function within the organization. A best practice is to have a compliance committee meet at least quarterly, and a best practice attendance mark is to have at least 75% of voting members in attendance. Although in-person attendance at the meeting is preferred, a committee member can call into the meeting or send a proxy in his or her place. The proxy holder should be another executive in the compliance committee member's operational function (e.g., the assistant chief financial officer when the chief financial officer is unable to be in attendance).

The compliance officer must have periodic access to key leaders in the organization. It is a best practice for the compliance officer to have regularly scheduled meetings with the CEO/president (e.g., quarterly) and with a key representative of the governing body.

In very large organizations, a best practice is to have a member of the governing body attend the compliance committee meetings. This ensures that the governing body is aware of the activities of the compliance committee, how the compliance function is fulfilled, and any significant compliance issues.

The member of the governing body who participates in the compliance committee can bring issues to the entire governing body that he or she believes are important for all board members to know.

Creating a Compliant Culture

It is one of the compliance officer's primary responsibilities to create, foster, and perpetuate a culture of compliance. If the compliance officer creates a culture of compliance, employees and constituents will work collaboratively to do the right thing.

To create a culture of compliance, the compliance officer needs to set the tone. The compliance officer should work as a facilitator to provide education and obtain the necessary resources for the organization to comply with all legal, regulatory, and mission requirements and objectives. The compliance officer must understand that most compliance issues arise because of misunderstandings of legal and regulatory requirements, lack of education, and lack of resources. A culture of compliance must be supported by appropriate resources. Compliance resources can include subscriptions to trade journals, attendance at conferences, and computerized resources like electronic billing.

Consider branding the compliance function. Using a logo or slogan can be a valuable culture-creating resource to constantly remind employees that they are interacting with the compliance program. Placing the logo or slogan on documents, and even the emails from the compliance department, can help promote the identity of the compliance function.

The creation and maintenance of a culture of compliance starts at the top. It is important that executive leadership, including the CEO, and the board emphasize the importance of compliance when appropriate. Employees should see executive leadership and the board speaking about and referencing the importance of compliance within the organization. However, executive leadership and the board must do more than "talk the talk"—they need to "walk the walk" of compliance. That is to say they must support compliance thought their actions, demonstrating to employees that they mean what they say. Part of a compliance effectiveness review, discussed later in this book, is to ask employees generally whether they believe that executive leadership and the board will act in a compliant manner even if such actions have a negative financial impact on the organization. As an example, do employees believe that executive leadership will support repayment of reimbursement received when it has determined that the organization did not meet all of the requirements to justify the retention of the reimbursement received? Also, do employees generally believe that executive leadership and the board will provide the compliance department with sufficient resources and recognition within the organization for the compliance department to carry out its duties in an effective and efficient manner?

It only takes one negative statement by the CEO to affect employees' perception of compliance within the organization. For example, the following statement at a leadership meeting from the CEO is a compliance culture killer: "We should not audit reimbursement we receive because if we perform audits, we may find potential billing or documentation errors. The rules are so complex and confusing. Besides, everyone makes billing mistakes."

Failing to respond in a timely manner to all compliance concerns, regardless of the source and whether the source is anonymous, can also negatively impact the culture of compliance. If employees are aware that compliance issues have been brought to the attention of the organization yet were not thoroughly vetted in a timely manner, this may lead employees to believe that although compliance encourages reporting, they will not be taken seriously. When it comes to fostering a compliant culture, actions truly speak louder than words.

The compliance officer, and the department as a whole, must be careful to confront compliance issues with the right demeanor. The compliance officer should remain objective until the facts, through appropriate investigation and review, are determined. Compliance officers should not jump to rash conclusions—doing so may harm the compliance officer's effectiveness and reputation. If the compliance officer routinely overreacts to potential risks, the organization, and especially executive leadership, may not take the compliance officer seriously when a major compliance concern is reported or alleged. Further, compliance officers should not take a "gotcha" approach. Such an attitude can negatively affect the compliance officer's reputation and may make employees reluctant to come forward with compliance concerns.

An impartial demeanor is also important when the compliance officer is interacting with the compliance reporter. The compliance officer should empathize with the compliance reporter but should not send the signal to the compliance reporter that the issue is presumed to be legitimate. The compliance officer should not give the impression that an investigation will be carried out with any bias.

Another best practice to foster a culture of compliance is to disclose the results of compliance reviews and investigations whenever possible. This includes making closure reports to the person who reported the compliance concern or through a closure report released via the organization's hotline. The compliance officer should also disclose the issues identified in a compliance review/investigation with the compliance committee. There are circumstances, such as when human resources issues are being investigated and resolved, when it may not be possible to disclose all details. Nevertheless, transparency, when and where appropriate, can help to foster a culture of compliance.

Even if an organization has a well-written code of compliance and policies and procedures, a compliance program will not be effective if the organization does not have a culture of compliance.

Chapter 8

The Risk Assessment

Risk is defined as the possibility that an event will occur that will adversely affect the achievement of objectives. Numerous internal and external risks can negatively affect the business intentions of management and the board. The healthcare industry is complex, and risk is everywhere. From patient safety risks to fraud and abuse risks, it is important to understand the significant risks your organization faces and to implement appropriate safeguards to mitigate them. There is no such thing as a risk-free endeavor in the healthcare industry.

So why is it important to identify risk exposures? Doing so:

- Is part of a good internal control process
- Permits your organization to assess and incur risk in a strategic fashion
- Permits establishment of safeguards to control/mitigate risks
- Ensures effective and efficient use of resources
- Focuses your audit/compliance plan on the areas of greatest risk
- Demonstrates understanding of your organization's strategic plan and helps ensure the plan's success
- Helps eliminate/reduce the risk of untoward outcomes
- Provides management and the board with an independent evaluation of risks and controls and helps contribute to risk management, control, and governance
- Demonstrates understanding of the legal and regulatory environment in which your organization functions
- Provides management with training on risk and control awareness
- Helps your organization comply with the requirements of the Sarbanes-Oxley Act (SOX) (if applicable)
- Is good business practice
- Decreases potential for negative public disclosure

The Importance of Risk Assessments

The complexity and competitiveness of today's business environment require that organizations have early warning systems to identify times when they face certain risks. Compliance officers should be active participants in the organization's risk assessment process.

As though they were forecasting the weather, organizations should scan the enterprise's environment continuously for potential warning signs and constantly update management on whether any particular risk is likely to occur, what the probability of its occurrence is, and how it could affect the organization if the potential risks materialize. Use the organizational risk questionnaire found in this book's downloadable materials to get an overview of the organization and how its senior leaders perceive the risks it is managing and is due to face.

When provided with the information on the threat and degree of risk, senior leadership can evaluate the information and make reasonable judgments about what to do with the risk. These judgments can be used to address major risks that are more likely to affect the organization.

Use the sample quarterly report to the board of trustees to keep the board and executives apprised of the changing risk profile (Figure 8.1). This quarterly report is also part of the downloadable tools available for this book.

FIGURE 8.1

QUARTERLY REPORT TO THE BOARD OF TRUSTEES

Note: Use this template to keep the board and executives apprised of the changing risk profile
Organization name: ______________________________
Period covered: ______________________________

1. Current compliance reviews.
   a) External reviews/audits/investigations.
   b) Internal reviews/self-disclosures.

2. Significant internal prevention/detection/correction projects.

3. Internal audit compliance reviews.
   Topic/issue Status/follow-up
   ____
   ____

4. Report of contacts to direct and anonymous reporting mechanisms this quarter.
   Date Topic Resolution/disposition
   ____
   ____

5. Significant changes/work efforts in the following areas this quarter:
   - Compliance program staffing
   - Education
   - Policy development/revision
   - Compliance disciplinary and/or reward mechanisms

Without a method of gathering this information, management is less likely to anticipate or mitigate risk. This shortcoming is a key element in the poor performance of many healthcare organizations.

In fact, an examination of companies that have had bad legal or compliance experiences may reveal that they lacked a robust organizational framework for assessing and managing risk, thus hindering their management of the risks they faced.

The Role of Risk Management

Two of the greatest impediments to business success are unrecognized risk and unmanaged risk. To address these barriers, the risk universe—that is, the variety and extent of possible risks the entity has—must be identified. Then, when the risk universe has been identified, the risks must be assessed for their likelihood and probability of occurrence. Those that seem most likely to occur and that would have the greatest negative effect on the entity should be managed through proper planning and control measures to keep the risks within reasonable and manageable parameters. This process is called risk mitigation.

Organizations that have adopted risk assessment and best practices usually identify risks in an organized manner. Having recognized that risk is a constant presence in the business environment that cannot be completely eliminated, they nevertheless understand that most risks can be contained within reasonable limits so as not to become detrimental to the entity.

In some organizations, risk management has been narrow—that is, it has focused heavily on controlling financial transactions. But organizations must expand their scope of risk management to include the entire business enterprise, from board governance to the business's transactional activities, including quality of care.

Compliance, risk management, and internal audit

The internal audit, risk management, and corporate compliance departments are partners in an organization's risk governance. Specifically, they present the outcome of the risk assessment process, help to prioritize risks, and help to identify and provide the resources necessary to mitigate those risks.

Once the universe of risk has been defined and information has been gathered, the risks need to be evaluated objectively. This process verifies the existence of the risk and assesses its extent, allowing the risk to be prioritized. Leaders of the organization can then make reasonably informed decisions and answer such questions as the following:

- Where are our greatest risks?
- Which risks are financial, quality-based, mission-based, legal, related to competition, reputational, or related to emergency preparedness?
- Who has oversight for the identified risks?

- What is being done about these risks?
- Is there sufficient information, and was it received in a timely manner?
- Has the proper amount of resources been allocated to manage these risks?
- Are the right resources involved?
- What risk mitigation activity needs to occur?
- What monitoring, auditing, and reporting are needed?
- What should be audited, and how often should it be audited?
- Which risks can be allowed to continue?
- Can an audit be performed with internal resources, or should external resources be used?

For a sample risk assessment worksheet, as well as an audit and compliance work plan, refer to the downloadable files for this book.

Auditors, risk managers, and compliance officers can help answer some of those questions. Their task is to develop a process to identify exposures within their organization and to determine whether mitigating controls are in place to reduce/eliminate the exposure. This task, however, is not always simple. It requires a clear understanding of the organization's inner workings and of the regulatory environment in which the organization functions. It asks a simple question: "What could go wrong?" In the healthcare context, the answer can include the following:

- Harm to the patient/substandard quality
- Financial loss/fines/penalties
- Adverse publicity
- Loss of referrals
- Investigation by an external organization (e.g., the Centers for Medicare & Medicaid Services [CMS], the Office of Inspector General [OIG], the Department of Justice [DOJ])
- Disasters/emergencies
- Criminal prosecution
- Exclusion from the Medicare/Medicaid programs

Government Focus on Risk Management

Even before highly publicized scandals in the for-profit and nonprofit sectors (e.g., Enron, WorldCom, HealthSouth, HCA, Tenet Health, and Tyco), which highlighted the need to identify risks, risk identification was an essential ingredient for those working in internal audit and compliance. In fact, the Institute of Internal Auditors International Standards for the Professional Practice of Internal Audit, under Standard 2110 Risk Management, states, "The internal audit activity should assist the organization by identifying and evaluating significant exposures to risk and contributing to the improvement of risk management and control systems."

Likewise, the government notes the importance of risk assessments in the *United States Sentencing Commission Guidelines Manual* (first adopted in 1987, and as amended on November 1, 2018), under section §8B2.1(c), as follows:

> *In implementing subsection (b), the organization shall periodically assess the risk of criminal conduct and shall take appropriate steps to design, implement, or modify each requirement set forth in subsection (b) to reduce the risk of criminal conduct identified through this process.*

The Sentencing Commission elaborated on risk assessments regarding "Effective Compliance Programs" in their Amendments to the Sentencing Guidelines, effective November 1, 2004, 69 *FR* 28994, 29023 (May 19, 2004), as follows:

> *In addition to the seven requirements for a compliance and ethics program, § 8B2.1(c) expressly provides, as an essential component of the design, implementation, and modification of an effective program, that an organization must periodically assess the risk of the occurrence of criminal conduct. The new guideline includes at Application Note 6 various factors that should be addressed when assessing relevant risks. Specifically, organizations should evaluate the nature and seriousness of potential criminal conduct, the likelihood that certain criminal conduct may occur because of the nature of the organization's business, and the prior history of the organization. To be effective, this process must be ongoing. Organizations must periodically prioritize their compliance and ethics resources to target those potential criminal activities that pose the greatest threat in light of the risks identified.*

Risk Management and Compliance Working Together

Risk management and compliance professionals should identify, assess, and address risks in a collaborative manner. Although their focus often is not the same as one another's, each is responsible for handling enterprisewide risk exposures. They should work in a supportive and collaborative way on many issues, and referral from one to the other should be ongoing.

In some states, risk management enjoys the privilege of confidentiality, and to use that protection, one must involve risk managers in any investigation. When looking at clinical risks, if there is a standard-of-care issue, both risk management and compliance should, at the commencement of the investigation, discuss how and by whom it will be investigated and handled.

Over time, the relationship between compliance and risk management should develop to a point where patterns of potential substandard care recognized through incident report trends or asserted claims are brought to the attention of the compliance officer, and potential problems identified through the anonymous hotline or compliance audits are shared with risk management.

Because these two functions need to work so closely together, risk management staff members should develop and maintain a working knowledge of the compliance field in general, the OIG *Work Plan,* and the organization's compliance plan to help keep the compliance officer advised of relevant issues.

Likewise, the compliance officer should have a working knowledge of risk management principles and issues of risk exposure to guide the communication of exposures or potentially compensable events that are identified in routine compliance activities.

Identifying Risks

The process of identifying risks does not have to be costly—one often can do so by reading industry publication headlines. For example, nonprofit hospital systems have faced class action lawsuits for their methods of billing and collecting from uninsured patients. Hospital systems have recently settled multimillion dollar *qui tam* allegations related to inappropriate financial arrangements with referral sources, including physicians. Perhaps these risks should be added to your organization's risk universe. Although the process of identifying possible risk exposures does not have to be costly, it does need to be documented through a formal process. This documentation should be maintained as proof of the organization's risk assessment process.

Risk is the possibility that an event will occur that adversely affects the achievement of objectives. In healthcare, the objective is to provide quality healthcare to those who need treatment. Identification of risks begins with gaining a clear understanding of the organization's operations. That is, is the organization an acute care hospital, a physician group, a rehabilitation hospital, or a home health agency? Is it part of an integrated healthcare delivery system? Each type of organization faces similar—albeit different—risks.

Resources for risk identification

You may be approaching an organization's risk exposures because you have recently assumed the position of compliance officer, either as a new hire or as a transfer from a different organizational role. In either case, gather some basic information to help identify risk exposures from the business and clinical perspectives.

First, review current literature targeted to your organization type as well as industry publications. These publications provide excellent summaries of hot topics from the hospital industry and the federal government.

Another relatively inexpensive way of identifying risk exposure is to network with peers and join a professional organization, such as the Association of Healthcare Internal Auditors, the Institute of Internal Auditors, and the Health Care Compliance Association. These organizations are both national and regional, so they allow members to network with local peers and attend reasonably priced seminars.

Attending a national or regional chapter-sponsored event not only provides members with up-to-date information on risks within your industry but also allows them to network and make invaluable contacts. These organizations often have chat rooms and listservs where members can post questions and receive email updates on hot topics. These organizations also have publications that identify risk areas and contain articles written by industry thought leaders.

Other entities as resources

There's no need to reinvent the wheel. Compliance officers can (and should) contact compliance officers from other entities to seek guidance regarding what risk issues they are reviewing.

External auditors

External auditors are excellent resources for identifying financial, operational, and compliance risks and for evaluating internal controls established by management to mitigate these risks. Doing so is extremely important to for-profit entities, especially with the emphasis that SOX places on internal controls.

OIG resources

Another invaluable resource in identifying risk exposures is the federal government—specifically, the OIG. The OIG website has opinion letters, guidance, and fraud alerts that can be used to identify risk areas the office is focusing on, as well as the OIG's opinion on those risk areas. The OIG's *Work Plan* is another valuable list of potential risks for healthcare entities.

Documentation

Documentation is essential to effectively recognizing risk areas. Obtaining available documentation to help pinpoint the organization's risk areas ensures that the organization's activities will focus on areas of greatest concern and that the documentation will support areas included in the organizational work plan. Use the following list of resources to identify areas of risk in the organization. This list is not all-inclusive and is in no particular order:

- Strategic plans
- Organizational charts
- Internal audit reports
- Hotline reports
- Occurrence reports
- Malpractice claims reports
- Clinical quality or patient satisfaction reports
- External audit reports
- OIG audit reports
- OIG compliance program guidance
- SOX guidance

Beyond the Basics of Identifying High-Risk Activities

One approach to performing risk assessments is to take an "enterprise risk assessment"—a comprehensive look at all departments and activities in your facility. It's a huge but necessary undertaking. Conducting this type of risk assessment means examining a full set of perspectives to understand the interrelationships between risk indicators and to determine risk mitigation and control activities.

To accomplish this task, take the following nine steps:

1. Identify subject matter experts. Make a list of everyone at your facility with whom you'll need to talk when seeking out high-risk areas. Executive management may be a good place to start, but don't limit your list. Those who actually perform high-risk tasks (e.g., billers, coders, medical record staff members, and registration personnel) will provide you with valuable insight on day-to-day risks.
2. Conduct interviews. Once you have identified your experts, decide the best way to find out what they know. There are several ways to conduct this process, including face-to-face interviews, surveys, and group meetings.

3. Review industry documents. Obtain and review recent OIG/CMS audit results and settlements, as well as Medicare and other industry-specific publications. Formulate questions that correspond with external audit trends. If an outside investigator shows up, you'll feel more confident if you can demonstrate that your facility has evaluated current issues.

4. Summarize risks. Summarize the most significant risks identified in interviews and industry documents. Compile these identified risks in a succinct, easy-to-understand format. This step not only helps you but also creates documents that are easy for others in your organization to follow, especially if you need to prove that you conducted the risk assessment.

5. Determine scope and make a preliminary list. After summarizing your risks, determine the scope of assessment needed for each item on the list. Doing so will help facilitate the identification of any risk-related data you need.

6. Identify data. Next, identify your organization's key compliance risk-related data. This step may be the most important area of your risk assessment and involves an intricate process. As you take this step, figure out what's most useful to you and to your organization—and, equally important, what information is most readily available. You may need to involve other departments, such as information technology, to obtain access to the needed information.

7. Finalize your list. For this step, decide the set of risks you will assess based on your interviews and data. To provide focus, share your preliminary list with others in your organization and solicit feedback. As when you conduct your preliminary interviews, do not limit your inquiry to executive management.

8. Evaluate control activities. Now that you have a solid preliminary list, you can start to predict which risks are the most urgent. To begin this process, evaluate controls already in place to mitigate potential risk. Return to your experts to help you determine a level for each risk. You can complete this step in several ways, including conducting group interviews, voting, soliciting email comments, or conducting one-on-one interviews. When assessing controls, consider the following three criteria:

   - The likelihood of an event. This means the inherent probability of risk occurring without considering existing controls.

   - The effect of a potential event. Assess the potential significance of a risk without considering existing controls. This may include, by way of example, the possible financial loss that may occur if the risk is not appropriately mitigated.

   - The existing risk factor. This refers to the estimated percentage of unmitigated risk when considering existing controls.

9. Calculate risk concern level and rank risk area. Use a matrix to create a final, formularized ranking for your risk areas. Although there is no single generally accepted approach to this step, the following process could be helpful:

   - Begin by gathering a group of knowledgeable personnel—either your compliance committee or a panel of trusted experts—to evaluate each item on the list. Ask the group to assign each item a 1–10 rating for both the likelihood of the risk and the potential effect of the risk.

   - Next, rely on the team to help calculate the item's risk factor. The risk factor is 100% minus your confidence level that control activities or other factors are effectively mitigating the risk. Your confidence level is a subjective percentage that you assign based on the perceived degree of risk.

   - Consider using an outside resource, such as a consultant who assigns risk to other clients on a daily basis. Finalize this process by showing your results in a graph format, with effect and likelihood in one quadrant and risk concern level in the other. This graph will help explain the process you used to arrive at the results. Lastly, have managers and others in your facility review the results to verify that everyone is on the same page. This process will depend on the culture of your organization.

Interviews and Questionnaires

One of the best ways to obtain information about the risk exposures facing an organization is to conduct walk-around interviews with department managers and staff members. The benefits of doing so can be significant. To prepare for such an interview, perform the following steps:

1. Obtain an organizational chart. Doing so will help identify where the interviewee's department sits in the organization's structure and to whom in the organization employees report.
2. Notify the interviewee's supervisor/manager. Unless you are conducting a surprise walk-around interview, contact the interviewee's supervisor/manager to let him or her know that you will be conducting an interview with the employee. Tell the manager the purpose of the interview and what you will do with the information you gather.
3. Obtain the interviewee's job description. Many interviewees may not have been provided with a job description upon hire. The job description serves many purposes, including the following:

   - Helping you understand what the interviewee's duties entail

   - Allowing you to notice whether the duties being performed by the individual are different from those in the job description

  - Serving as a standard against which to judge the individual's performance, which any supervisor/manager needs in order to conduct an effective performance appraisal

  - Indicating the employee's influence over identified risks or involvement in mitigating processes

4. Prepare. Walk-around interviews disrupt both the department in which you conduct the interview and the employee you interview. To minimize disruption, be prepared for the interview. Have a good understanding of the department's workflow, have your questions prepared in advance, inform the interviewee of the purpose of the interview, and make him or her feel at ease.

Once you understand the interviewee's job function, understand the department's workflow, and have identified a good time to visit with the individual, arrange for and conduct the interview itself. Be punctual to make good use of the interview time.

To obtain the best-quality answers and information, you will need to assure all respondents that their individual answers are confidential. Thus, a nonretaliation policy is important for the success of your compliance program.

Risk Questionnaire

The most important part of a risk assessment is what you do with the information you collect and how you convert it into an effective plan that will mitigate business risks.

Collect the information by interviewing most of the organization's key managers and asking them to respond to questions about the organization and their area of management responsibility. This methodology allows you to add risk questions specific to the organization or a specific department or to delete questions that do not fit the organization.

The power of this approach is that the answers come from those who know the organization best. When all of management's answers are aggregated, they should paint a solid picture of management's perspective of the organization and of those risk areas that may require attention. The questions should focus on both the organization's perspective and the department's perspective.

You may arrange the questions in any sequence you wish, although the best answers often come from asking general questions first and then moving to the department-specific questions. Because of the personal investment the respondent has in his or her area of responsibility, approaching questions related to it later in the interview tends to result in better-quality responses. Make sure that the questions are open-ended, not accusatory or based on assumptions.

Six Approaches to Managing Risk

There are six generic approaches to managing risk, and the approach an organization chooses to use will depend on many factors. For example, how real is this risk? Can it actually become a problem, or is it merely theoretical? Management will want to decide whether the risk is likely to happen and whether it is possible to determine when it may happen. This will also assist in appropriate allocation of resources to focus on those risk areas that are material.

During this process, management will likely choose from six options:

1. Risk can be accepted. As long as it is not an undue risk, it can be accepted as an inherent part of being open for business. The existing mechanisms that are in place may be sufficient to manage the risk. In fact, without accepting risk, all business would grind to a standstill. Companies that do not move forward or that fail to adequately manage the increased risk see themselves outdistanced by their competitors.
2. Risk can be controlled. In this common approach, with some adjustments, the new risk can be brought within acceptable limits. Resources are deployed, capabilities are increased, additional control measures are installed, monitoring is improved, auditing is stepped up, reporting is made more comprehensive and timely, policies and procedures are enhanced, and so on.
3. Risk can be diversified. Often, risks can be brought within acceptable limits by changing the existing processes. For example, you can redesign or break the process into component parts, find and use multiple sources for supplies, distribute production to more than one location, co-source certain components, change business contracts and relationships, etc.
4. Risk can be shared. The most common sharing arrangement is insuring the risk. Buying an insurance policy to cover part or all of a risk can distribute the financial consequence of an unanticipated event. Examples include insurance for fraud allegation; business cessation insurance for catastrophic losses such as fires, hurricanes, and tornados; and cybersecurity insurance. Sharing with a partner is another way to share risk. Partners can financially share in negative outcomes and provide resources and experiences to joint ventures.
5. Risk can be transferred. Companies can find someone else who is willing or better able to take on a particular task, usually for a premium price. In these cases, allowing the other party to assume the risk is the better alternative. Examples include outsourcing the billing or legal functions.
6. It is not always necessary to accept risk. Instead, you can avoid it in several ways:
    - Management can cease and desist the service or activity
    - Change management or service provider (e.g., engage new laboratory)
    - Product or service lines may be dropped because of the high risks they carry
    - Part of the business can be sold or closed if the risk is too high

- A service line can be joint ventured with another entity
- Decisions to get around the risk can be made

Risk management is a major consideration in business. The most successful companies tend to be those that understand the probable consequences of risk to their organization. They respond by establishing an adaptable process within their business structure that scans their environment for risks and determines the best means of mitigating those risks. By doing so, they keep the entity within the limits of controlled risk that are reasonable for their current situation.

Chapter 9

Training Strategies

Education and training are critical components of an effective compliance plan. Training and education set the tone for the compliance program and the ethics of the organization. In addition, effective education helps in meeting the training criteria of the Federal Sentencing Guidelines, which state that the organization should take reasonable steps to periodically and practically communicate its standards, procedures, and other aspects of the compliance and ethics program. The information should be appropriate to individuals' respective roles and responsibilities.

Training also serves as a preventive control, which can be an important component for meeting external financial audit expectations, including the entity-level controls that are required as part of Sarbanes-Oxley for public companies.

This chapter will discuss and review current training programs and methods and explain how to develop and evaluate new training programs and methods.

Scope of Training

The scope of the training for the compliance program will depend on many factors. Each compliance officer may have a different group or depth of regulations for which he or she is responsible. The compliance officer should develop a comprehensive list of the regulatory risk areas that will be used as a guide when developing the compliance training plan. Initially, many compliance programs may focus on only billing and coding or only Anti-Kickback and Stark laws. As the compliance program matures, other in-depth areas can be targeted for education.

Another topic related to scope of training is the depth of that training, which differs based on the level of risk exposure. In some cases, the only training needed may be awareness that a regulation exists and basic guidance about whom to call if an employee has questions. Alternatively, an employee in another position may need to understand the details of the regulation to compliantly conduct his or her responsibilities.

For example, there are laws surrounding what gifts may be given to a public official. Most employees in their normal course of business will not have a reason to offer such gifts, so the basic guidance may be to provide general education regarding the prohibitions related to gifts to public officials, with direction to contact the head of government affairs (if there is an individual in this role) or the legal or compliance department if the situation occurs.

In other cases, if it becomes an active goal of the organization to have public officials visit the organization or to visit such individuals at their office, in-depth training may be provided to the personnel who make decisions about the visits.

Another example is how an organization handles compliance with the nonmonetary compensation exception under the Stark Law. Employees who do not give out any nonmonetary benefits to referring physicians may need to know only the existence of restrictions that are placed on the giving of such benefits. Alternatively, executives who *do* give out nonmonetary benefits (i.e., dinners at local restaurants, tickets to sporting events) will need to know the annual limit for such benefits and how the organization tracks the benefits to ensure that all of the benefits given out during a calendar year do not exceed the applicable annual limit. This is especially true for C-suite executives and members of the finance department who are responsible for tracking such benefits.

It may not always be necessary for everyone to understand the intricacies of the regulations. Instead, detailed training can be conducted on the policies and procedures written to encompass details of the regulations. For example, there are a multitude of claim edits for Medicare billing. It is probably not essential that everyone know all of the potential claim edits, but employees should understand that there is a system in place to screen billed services that is based on Centers for Medicare & Medicaid Services requirements. Conceptually, this would be spelled out in an organization's billing policies. Of course, the person developing the training must understand the regulations and any controls, automated or manual, that are built into the system.

From a compliance perspective, there are two general categories of compliance training: training related to the organization's internal compliance program and training related to job-specific responsibilities.

Compliance program training

Training regarding the structure and elements of the organization's compliance program should include recognition of the existence of the compliance program, the code of conduct, the organization's nonretaliation policy, and how to bring an issue to the organization's attention by speaking with a supervisor, consulting the compliance officer, or calling the hotline. Such training should occur at new employee orientation and at least annually thereafter. Effective compliance programs also continue to emphasize these components periodically through articles in employee newsletters, posters, screensavers, or other promotional avenues. In addition, effective programs attempt to brand themselves through the use of symbols or slogans. One branding and compliance education resource that has received national recognition is Captain Integrity, which can be found at *www.captainintegrity.com.*

General compliance training should also focus on high-risk legal and regulatory requirements. This includes general training regarding the requirements and restrictions under the Anti-Kickback Statute, Stark Law, Civil Monetary Penalties, False Claims Act, and Health Insurance Portability and Accountability Act of 1996 (HIPAA). Some sectors of the healthcare industry may also have dominant legal and regulatory requirements, including research requirements, Food and Drug Administration requirements, and laws and regulations that impact healthcare entities that manufacture or sell devices or pharmaceuticals internationally. The scope of training regarding these legal and regulatory requirements will depend upon the participants receiving the training. At a minimum, everyone within an organization should be educated regarding the major legal and regulatory issues impacting the organization. This will ensure that participants are aware of the existence of the requirements and understand that the organization will implement policies and procedures and conduct business in compliance with the requirements.

Training for job-specific compliance

The second category of compliance education is education directed toward the employee's specific job responsibility. As noted above, such education will need to identify either the existence of applicable laws or regulations or, depending upon the employee's area of responsibility, a detailed analysis of such laws and regulations.

By way of example, physicians who supervise nonphysician providers need to understand the regulations that apply to such supervision as well as the billing requirements for the nonphysician provider's services. If the physician intends to bill the nonphysician provider's services "incident to" the physician's services, the physician will need to know and understand that the physician is required to see the patient for the initial visit and establish a plan of care, whereas the nonphysician provider can see the patient independently for follow-up visits. The nonphysician provider's services can either be billed directly using the nonphysician provider's provider number or billed using the physician's provider number as long as the physician is in the office suite when the nonphysician provider sees the patient.

Who Should Be Trained?

Employees will always require training. Nonemployee workforce members who interact with or provide services on behalf of the organization also require special consideration. HIPAA defines "workforce" as employees, contractors, volunteers, trainees, and others whose conduct, in the performance of work for the organization, is under the direct control of the organization, regardless of whether they are paid by the organization. Under this definition, many people would require training, including temporary workers who supplement an organization's regular workforce. In this case, some training responsibilities should be written into the contract for the subcontractor to perform and certify.

One common concern in healthcare provider organizations is whether training is needed for medical staff members who are not employed by the organization. This may include physicians as well as other allied health professionals, such as nurse practitioners and orthotists. The answer may be covered in the organization's medical staff bylaws. However, most effective compliance programs require periodic training for independent members of its medical staff so that these members know and understand the organization's compliance program as well as all laws and regulations that impact the independent medical staff's interactions with the organization.

By way of example, it may be beneficial to provide training on the Stark Law to all members of the medical staff so that they understand the restrictions that are applicable to all financial arrangements between the medical staff members and the hospital. It is more productive for medical staff members to know that there is a law restricting their financial arrangements than for them to believe that the hospital is making up rules to limit financial arrangements with its referring physicians.

Likewise, a device manufacturer or pharmaceutical entity should provide training to its independent contractors, including the sales force. These manufacturers assume risk through the activities of their contractors because the third parties believe that the contractors are representatives, and therefore agents, of the manufacturer. These manufacturers may also have physician consultants who must be trained on the legal and regulatory issues, such as the Anti-Kickback Statute, that impact the physicians' consulting services.

Frequency and Timing of Training

There are a few considerations when looking at the frequency of training. First is the regulatory angle—some regulations require certain employees to have training. For example, HIPAA's Privacy and Security rules require that all members of a covered entity's workforce receive training at the time of or before the full implementation of any new regulation. It also requires that new workforce members receive training. In this case, the workforce includes more than just employees.

Second, people are often trained upon entering the organization. This practice, aside from being efficient, sets the tone and informs the trainees of where to turn with questions. Thus, it is important to decide what new employees need to know immediately upon hire (i.e., before productive hours ever happen) versus what is more useful and will be remembered after they have had some exposure to the job.

For example, if you begin the training of a new billing person with complicated and technical material, such as working system edits, without letting the person become familiar with the basics, he or she may not be able to retain the information. In cases where a person is changing his or her type of work (e.g., moving from a clinical position to a clinical liaison role in the business office) or just starting a job in the healthcare industry, this issue of timing and frequency becomes even more critical, as the new hire's previous level of exposure to the regulations may not be adequate to ensure compliance in the new position.

Finally, once a person has gone through the initial training, how often does refresher training need to occur? Often, it is performed annually, although refresher training may cover new issues on the same topic. For example, timing the refresher training for coding and billing to coincide with final rules in the fall will be advantageous for the organization.

There are many opportunities to deliver compliance training at various points in the employee's tenure with the organization. If the organization is committed to ensuring compliance, this message can be delivered at new employee orientation, sessions targeted at subcontractors, annual required education or benefit fairs, or mandatory computer-based training programs; written into the organization's global policies and procedures; or included in preceptorship programs for individuals changing positions within the organization.

As noted above, an effective means of emphasizing the existence of an organization's compliance program is through branding with a symbol or a slogan. Logos and slogans are training vehicles, as they constantly remind employees of the existence of the compliance program. By branding your compliance program, whenever an employee sees the slogan or symbol, they will be reminded, possibly daily, of the existence of the compliance program. If the compliance program is only "rolled out" once a year, retention of any educational material may be diminished.

Employees can get another daily reminder of the program's existence by seeing that the compliance officer is actively reviewing and investigating issues and bringing issues to closure. Even though the active involvement of a compliance officer is not deemed to be traditional training and education, it definitely is a visible sign of the organization's emphasis on conducting business ethically and in compliance with all applicable laws, rules, and regulations.

Training gap analysis

One way of reviewing the scope of training is to conduct a training gap analysis by identifying applicable regulations and how they are covered by the organization. Gap analyses formally identify the gaps between desired and actual levels of performance in a particular area. In this case, they compare the desired level of understanding of the regulations to the actual training and education available within the organization. See Figure 9.1 for a form to use in reviewing which training courses cover which regulatory material. This tool can also be found in the downloadable material for this book.

FIGURE 9.1

Training Gap Analysis

A=General B=In-depth

	Training course				
Regulatory knowledge area	**Compliance orientation**	**Compliance refresher**	**Coding**	**Referral source relationships**	**Releasing EOBs**
HIPAA	A	A			B
False Claims					
Anti-kickback	A			B	
Stark				B	

Role analysis

Another component of evaluating training programs is to review role analysis: who undergoes what training. Although there may be some compliance training that everyone needs, much of the training will be limited to certain personnel depending upon their role. It is possible for an employee to have several roles within the organization; some may be formally defined, others merely understood. See Figure 9.2 for a sample form to use when completing a role analysis (it is also available in the book's downloadable material).

For each role in the organization, you will determine which courses are mandatory and which are optional. The roles may be defined by supervision level and functional area. For employees with multiple roles, therefore, training requirements for each role would be combined when reviewing their required courses.

FIGURE 9.2

Training Role Analysis

A=Mandatory B=Optional

	Training course				
Role	Compliance orientation	Compliance refresher	Coding	Referral source relationships	Releasing EOBs
Nonsupervisory nursing	A	A			B
Therapy					
Business office					
Senior management					

In the role analysis, also consider the roles that may be played by someone who is not an employee of the organization. This is especially true with the governing body of the organization (i.e., board of trustees). Many board members are visible community leaders with no healthcare experience. By way of example, if a board member is the CEO of a bank, he or she may not understand the intricacies of the Anti-Kickback Statute, Stark Law, or False Claims Act that apply to the healthcare industry.

Because the board is responsible for general oversight of the organization's compliance program, including ensuring that sufficient resources are dedicated to the operation of the compliance function, board education on compliance issues is very important.

Training Development

Now that training gaps have been identified, training development can begin. Some topics to consider here are subject matter experts, training delivery method, and the use of outside vendors.

Subject matter experts

One of the first tasks is to identify subject matter experts within the organization. These experts may already reside within the compliance department in some cases. The compliance department should consider getting personnel to assist in reviewing the language of the training and developing pertinent examples to bring the material to life. Many people will better remember training that includes examples applicable to their role.

By way of example, if the training is to teach clinicians about appropriate medical record documentation, a poorly documented medical record could be used as part of the education (with protected health information deleted to comply with HIPAA).

Method of delivery

Another aspect to consider early in the process is the delivery method of the training, whether in person, by computer, or through some other variation. In-person training allows people to ask questions as the material is delivered, and a skillful trainer can identify confusion and explain or repeat information as needed. However, in many cases, the cost of in-person training is higher than that for other methodologies. Ensure that the training is not delivered via a lecture format in which people can easily tune out the trainer. Some in-person training methods, such as knowledge maps, allow for an interactive group format with nonconfrontational learning about difficult subjects.

Computer training can take many forms, from PowerPoint presentations, to live sessions recorded for later replay, to video- or other scenario-based learning. One of the big advantages to computer training is the consistency of its delivery, which ensures that the same message is given throughout the organization.

Use of outside vendors

Ultimately, the training budget may determine whether outside vendors are used for training. Many vendors have prepackaged training available for purchase. Each degree of customization will have an incremental cost to the organization; however, customizing the training with language and scenarios that personnel recognize can greatly facilitate their absorption of the material. The compliance officer may also identify effective trainers at compliance conferences he or she attends. Frequently, fellow compliance officers, lawyers, and consultants are willing to come to organizations to provide on-site training.

Sometimes using outside resources can effectively confirm the positions taken by the compliance officer. Due to the complex state of the regulations applicable to the healthcare industry, many times, business leaders do not believe that the compliance officer's stance on certain issues is correct. By engaging people outside of the organization to provide training and education, the position taken by the compliance officer may be affirmed.

General Compliance Training

When developing general training, often called compliance orientation training, one of the items to address is the scope of the training in terms of ethics and compliance. Ethics is the system of moral principles or rules of conduct related to a particular organization. Compliance can be defined as obedience to laws, regulations, policies, or some form of authority. Compliance officers may be able to drive compliance with laws and regulation, but the CEO and the senior management ultimately drive the ethics and culture of the organization. Thus, the CEO needs to deliver this message through both words and actions.

Compliance orientation training should occur at least annually, but it should be exemplified on a daily basis through the conduct of the organization's executive leadership, the compliance officer, and the branding of the compliance program.

Many organizations also hold a Compliance Week during which the compliance officer can provide general compliance education. It is important to make Compliance Week fun by offering giveaways or token items (e.g., coffee mugs, pens, notepads) that emphasize the compliance program, including the contact number for the compliance officer and the organization's hotline.

Specific training

Many topics will need to be covered in training that are specific to smaller groups of personnel. In healthcare organizations, such topics commonly include the following:

- Medicare vs. Medicaid rules
- Compliance with Medicare's *Conditions of Participation*
- Local and national coverage determinations
- Case management and medical necessity
- Anti-Kickback Statute
- Stark Law
- False Claims Act
- HIPAA
- Employment laws and regulations
- The Emergency Treatment and Active Labor Act
- Cost report requirements
- Nonphysician provider supervision ("incident to" and shared/split service)

Sometimes, when developing training on specific topics, it may help to audit the topic first to determine which areas need reinforcement. This can be especially helpful in billing and coding.

Training Evaluation

Once the training program is in place, it is time to evaluate its effectiveness. This measurement may be a combination of retention and evaluation. Depending on the course material, there may be a test immediately following course completion, with a specific score required to get credit for the course. Retention can also be tested at a later point without affecting credit. This can assist in developing tools for long-term retention of information. See Figure 9.3 for a form to use when evaluating the training methods at your facility. (The evaluation form is also part of this book's downloadable tools.)

FIGURE 9.3

Training Evaluation Form

	Strongly disagree	Disagree	No opinion	Agree	Strongly agree
The information presented . . . was accurate					
. . . was timely					
Presenter was professional					
. . . was prepared					
. . . was understandable					
Material was informative					
Format was easy to use					
Educational goals related to the topic were met					
I understand the regulations related to . . .					
I understand the policies related to . . .					

With the tools discussed in this chapter, the organization can review its training programs to assess coverage and effectiveness. In some cases, the organization may use only part of the tools to refresh and review the training programs. It is important for the compliance officer to consider how the compliance training fits into the provider's larger training and organizational development plan. Compliance elements can also be integrated into other training at the organization.

If the compliance training program is ever questioned, such as when conducting a compliance effectiveness review or as part of defending the effectiveness of the compliance program in a government investigation, the organization will need to provide documentation substantiating the effectiveness of the training. The best way to do so is to track all compliance training and retain tracking logs. Tracking should include what type of training was provided, when it was provided, who participated, and whether participants completed the training.

The individual or department responsible for tracking compliance training will depend on the resources of the organization. At smaller organizations, it may be conducted by the compliance officer or the compliance department. At larger organizations, compliance training can be tracked through the organization's education department. If the education department is responsible for tracking compliance training, the compliance officer must know what training modules or other elements are designated as "compliance." If the tracking systems permit, it is a best practice to designate training as part of either the compliance program's general compliance training or its role-specific compliance training.

The compliance officer should test the tracking mechanisms by periodically asking for documentation.

Tracking resources can be used by the compliance officer to monitor training deadlines and completion. A training deficiency report can assist the compliance officer in identifying who has not received assigned/required training. By way of example, if every employee and contractor is required to complete annual general compliance training, the compliance officer can, through the tracking mechanism, determine which employees or contractors have not completed it. The compliance officer can then provide reminders to those employees and contractors as well as to their supervisors.

The board should be informed of the organization's compliance training program and the percentage of employees and contractors who have completed it. By way of example, if all employees and contractors are required to complete a certain compliance training module but only 95% completed the module, the board should be notified of this shortfall. Board members should expect 100% completion, or an explanation, employee-by-employee, for why training was not completed. An example of an acceptable outlier may be a part-time employee who did not work during the assigned time to complete the assigned education. The board should be assured that the part-time employee will be required to complete the assigned education when and if he or she is called to work.

As the compliance officer, you should be prepared to answer the board's questions regarding the type, frequency, manner, and completion rate of compliance training.

Chapter 10

Monitoring and Auditing

A significant component of effective compliance programs as defined by the Federal Sentencing Guidelines is "monitoring and auditing to detect criminal conduct." In addition to detecting criminal conduct, most compliance programs also monitor and audit to detect errors that may not be intentional.

Given the complexity of regulation at the federal and state levels regarding billing and coding, unintentional billing errors can occur even in the most vigilant organization. A comprehensive audit program can help to detect these issues.

Understanding the Purposes of Monitoring and Auditing

In its *Compliance Program Guidance for Hospitals,* the Office of Inspector General (OIG) outlines its expectations for an effective healthcare compliance program, including monitoring and auditing of coding and billing for services rendered to government beneficiaries. The OIG recommends that providers perform audits of coded data at least annually and suggests that monitoring of coded data be performed on a regular basis.

Audits serve two very important purposes. First, they help to identify errors or patterns of error. Second, they serve as ongoing oversight of your organization's coding and billing functions.

There are distinct differences between auditing and monitoring. Auditing looks at the sample item (the unit being measured, such as billing claims or contract payment) in detail. Audits seek to determine whether the claims submitted are correct based on the services provided. Monitoring, on the other hand, seeks to determine whether necessary processes are being performed correctly. Monitoring usually occurs after errors or omissions are identified in audits. It ensures that safeguards or changes in processes that were implemented as a result of audit findings are effective and being followed.

A classic example of the difference between auditing and monitoring can be seen in credit balances. Credit balances can exist in any industry where bills are sent out and payment is expected. In healthcare, a credit balance is most often defined as a negative balance in a patient's accounts receivable that may be the result of an employee posting error (e.g., payment posted to the wrong account), an overpayment by a payer, or other reason. For example, the hospital submits a bill (e.g., UB-04) for a three-day acute care hospital stay. Based upon the contract with the payer, the hospital has an expected payment. When the actual payment is received from the payer, it is higher than what was expected, resulting in a credit balance. A typical hospital policy requires that any credit balances be reviewed every 30 days until resolved, which is defined as doing the research to determine whether the balance was caused by an improper posting of a contractual adjustment, a posting error to the wrong account, or an overpayment by the payer (who is thus owed a refund).

The illustration of monitoring versus auditing in this credit balance example is as follows:

- Monitoring. The amount of credit balances by payer is reported to the compliance committee each month. The ongoing review and reporting of credit balances to the compliance committee is the act of monitoring. The identified risk area (i.e., credit balance amount) is subject to an ongoing assessment to identify any positive or negative trends. If the trend shows an increasing amount of credit balances for any payer, remediation may be initiated.
    - This monitoring activity will not show the account moving from credit balance to resolved status (i.e., a $0 balance), or whether the proper decision was made regarding what caused the credit balance. The monitoring activity also will not show whether the proper remedial action occurred, which could include adjusting the payer contractual (e.g., the payment appeared to be more than was due but in reality was correct, perhaps due to a yearly increase), moving the payment to the proper account (e.g., the account was in credit balance status because the payment had been credited to the wrong account), or refunding money to the payer (e.g., in the case of an overpayment, thus refunding the payer through a claim adjustment or paper check). The monitoring activity reviews global trends in credit balances by payer to assess whether an audit is warranted.
- Auditing. If global or systemic trends are identified due to the organization's monitoring activities, an audit may be initiated. The auditor reviews a selection of accounts that had credit balances as of six months ago and answers the following questions:
    - Were accounts reviewed once every 30 days? If not, did the business office manager follow up with the responsible biller?
    - Was the proper decision made regarding the credit balances?
    - Based on the decision, did action occur as required by policy?

The auditor (especially if he or she is outside the compliance department) may also review whether the required reports were presented to the compliance committee and what actions the committee required if there were negative trends.

In the previous example, the auditing of the decision and action is especially important because no monitoring can determine whether the correct action took place for an individual account. Later in this chapter, potential additional methods of reviewing credit balances will be discussed.

Two of the common questions related to auditing in the compliance program are as follows:

- To whom should the audit personnel report?
- What specific personnel should perform the audits?

The answers to these questions will depend upon the size of the organization. Small organizations may not have the capacity for a separate audit function, so any audits may be performed by the compliance personnel or outsourced. If there are personnel assigned to a compliance audit function, they may report to the compliance officer or the head of internal audit for the organization, depending again on the structure of the organization and the authority level of the compliance officer.

The question about who should perform the audits is related to the question of whether the compliance audit function should be outsourced. Any audit has administrative aspects (e.g., gathering information from various places in the organization), and this can usually be performed at a lower cost if done in-house. Conversely, other parts of certain audits may require a very specific skill set (e.g., diagnosis coding), and such audits may require an external auditor due to the specialty-specific requirements, the scale of the audit function, or the number of audits currently taking place.

Determining the Overall Audit Plan

There are several steps in determining the overall audit and monitoring plan. Audit plans, ideally, should be developed annually, allowing flexibility for sporadic audits during the year when risk issues are identified. The first key step is to conduct a risk assessment, which can take many forms. Some organizations may use the OIG *Work Plan* as a basis for deciding which risk areas to include in the assessment. An organization may have a comprehensive list of risk areas from several regulatory agencies. The audit plan can also be established based upon reported issues that have impacted other organizations, especially organizations in the same healthcare industry sector. Compliance officers can learn what risk areas other organizations are auditing by networking with peers and attending conferences.

There are several factors, then, to consider when rating the risks. Generally, there is some type of scaling or weighting system, such as effect and probability. The effect factor may consider such things as the following:

- Financial exposure
- Legal exposure
- Potential for adverse publicity
- Potential for patient harm
- Potential for licensure/accreditation issues
- Potential for *qui tam* litigation
- History or issues involving the risk area (within the organization or the applicable healthcare sector)

The probability indicator may take into account the following:

- Level of work/findings by external auditors
- Level of work/findings by corporate internal audit services
- Quality of internal control environment
- Effectiveness of controls
- Time and findings since last review
- Experience of personnel with oversight authority
- Turnover in department
- Future acquisition
- Level of resources dedicated to risk area

Many organizations assign a numeric weight to each effect factor and probability indicator. By way of example, if a risk area will have a large effect on the organization and the probability of error is likewise large, the organization can assign a 5 to the effect factor and a 5 to the probability indicator (with 5 being the highest score). Thus, for this hypothetical risk factor, a weighted score of 25 would be assigned (5 effect × 5 probability = 25). The larger the weighted score, the greater the risk to the organization. Risk areas that are assigned the highest scores should be the subjects of your organization's annual audit plan.

Based on this risk assessment, the compliance department can choose the topics to include in the audit plan. Some topics may have only auditing or only monitoring activity; others may have both. Another factor to consider is whether a particular risk area is part of the core business of the entity—for example, billing for acute care stays (Medicare severity diagnosis-related groups [DRG]) for an acute care hospital—versus a one-off business for the organization (e.g., an acute care hospital with one small dialysis provider). A small service line such as this may not be much of the organization's revenue, but it also may not undergo as much scrutiny because fewer people in the organization are familiar with the risks associated with dialysis providers. Therefore, the highest revenue-producing risk areas may not always result in the highest quantified risk score.

Types of Audits

The next step in audit plan development is selecting the type of auditing or monitoring (monitoring will be covered later in the chapter). For billing and coding areas, there are generally two main types of audits: surveillance and outlier.

Surveillance audits can be defined as those in which the scope of the audit comprises similar items (sampling units), with a random sample of items selected for audit. Each item is reviewed against the applicable policies, regulations, and guidelines. For example, in an acute care hospital, a surveillance audit might encompass a random selection of all paid Medicare inpatient claims.

With outlier audits, data mining or analysis is used to try to identify anomalies. If anomalies are identified, further audits may be conducted. An example of outlier monitoring in acute care hospitals is the Centers for Medicare & Medicaid Services' (CMS) Program for Evaluating Payment Patterns Electronic Report (PEPPER), which is an electronic data report developed under contract by the Hospital Payment Monitoring Program Quality Improvement Organization Support Center.

PEPPER contains hospital-specific Medicare inpatient prospective payment system discharge data for target areas—specific DRG and discharges that have been identified as at high risk for payment errors in the short-term acute care hospital setting. When hospitals receive the data, the usage of a DRG code above a certain threshold (e.g., above the 75th percentile) could trigger a sample being selected for review to ensure that documentation is present to support all codes on the bill. This process compares your organization's billing frequency, by code, with the billing frequency of other hospitals. For each outlier type analysis, the threshold may or may not be predefined. The organization could choose to further review the extremes of the outlier ranking (e.g., the highest usage DRG, the highest payment).

It is important to note that in an outlier audit, the existence of an outlier does not necessarily indicate a problem. Depending on the business model, there are many legitimate reasons for an organization to have outliers, such as patient acuity mix, payer mix, and standards of practice in the community.

In other areas of audit, there may be questions about the auditing standard. One approach is to conduct the audit with the applicable policy as the standard, including each deviation from the policy as a finding.

In some cases, the audit may be conducted by legal experts. This is usually applicable when doing audits of contracts. The legal review would use the law as the standard. For example, if a healthcare provider was auditing relationships with physicians, there may be an analysis of Stark Law applicability and whether an exception is met as required by the law (if applicable). Often, these types of audits will be performed under attorney-client privilege.

The size and structure of the audit may also depend upon on whether the issue being audited is isolated or systemic. An isolated audit may only involve one code or procedure to determine whether your organization is billing for that procedure correctly. A systemic audit will test a broader spectrum of issues and claims to determine whether your organization has a larger issue. By way of example, a systemic review is one where a hospital looks at its inpatient billing processes and procedures based upon the DRGs billed to determine whether it is billing for inpatient services consistent with all legal and regulatory requirements.

Internal or External?

Once there is a decision about the audit plan (or perhaps even earlier in the process), there are decisions to be made about who will perform the audit.

The internal resources department (i.e., the compliance audit or internal audit) is the most common resource used and is usually the most cost-effective. To address specialty skill sets, some organizations may use internal resources outside of the audit department that do not have direct-line responsibility or, at a minimum, that do not audit their own department or functional area. The audit department may then choose to have some external validation of the audit results (i.e., an audit of the auditors) by selecting a small subsample of items for review.

At other times, if an organization does not have a particular specialty skill set, it may decide to outsource the audit. Some organizations choose to outsource the entire audit function. One advantage of outsourcing is that external auditors have more resources (e.g., personnel, comparison data, history with payers, electronic claims "scrubbers"). Sometimes, an organization or individual might believe that an interpretation of a regulation is correct and not identify a potential problem; in such a circumstance, an external source might have knowledge of subsequent modifications or clarifications to the regulation that were not identified by the organization.

Although outsourcing audits has its advantages, external auditors may be more costly and potentially more disruptive to your organization's operations because the external auditors may not have a working knowledge of how your organization operates or the personnel involved.

Universes and Sample Selection

Once audits are ready to be started, universes, populations, and sample selection methodology will need to be chosen. As the audit team begins planning, the universe of the data is the first thing to be considered. The universe determination assesses whether the claims are to be drawn from a specific code, department, provider, or date. This is a limited universe. A broader universe may include all claims by a payer for a longer period of time (e.g., all Medicare DRGs for one calendar year). The audit team will need to work with the owners of the data to determine such things as the following:

- Is there an electronic repository of information? For billing and coding audits, the answer is usually yes, but there may not be one for contractual arrangements, such as medical director contracts or outside-reference laboratory services.
- If there is an electronic repository, what data elements are available? For core businesses, such as inpatient services for an acute care hospital, all elements desired for selection may be available. If a business is noncore, such as a new home health agency started by an acute care hospital, there may be a more limited selection of elements. For example, the billing for a

new home health agency may be occurring electronically using software provided by CMS or a Medicare Administrative Contractor.

It is definitely to the advantage of the auditor to automatically populate as much data as possible from the electronic repository. This not only saves work but also eliminates some of the opportunity for human error in data entry.

At this stage, it is also critically important to determine whether the claims will be audited on a retrospective or prospective basis. A retrospective audit will review claims that have already been submitted and paid; any errors identified have to be corrected and repaid. A prospective audit will review claims prior to submission to the applicable payer; if any errors are identified, the errors can be corrected prior to submission of the claim to the applicable payer. Thus, in a prospective audit, no repayment of the claim is necessary because the claims reviewed have not been submitted to the applicable payer. However, depending upon the type of service being audited, there may be an insufficient number of claims to review on a prospective basis. If possible, conducting prospective audits of claims is preferable to conducting retrospective audits. If errors are found during a prospective audit, they can be corrected before the claim is submitted. However, if errors are found during a retrospective audit, it may be necessary to resubmit the impacted claims and calculate and return overpayments.

Now that the universe possibilities have been determined, the auditor will want to consider the size of the population for selection. Does the population consist of all the claims submitted in one year or in one month? Have the claims been coded but not yet billed? The advantage of this is that claims can be corrected before being submitted to a payer. The decision may depend upon factors such as the following:

- Timing since the last audit. For an annual surveillance audit, the population would likely cover the 12 months since the end date of the population from the previous audit.
- Timing of changes to the system. For example, CMS recently changed the physician supervision requirements for cardiac rehabilitation performed on a hospital campus. Any audits for the appropriate location of the supervising physician should be timed to coincide with the change implemented by CMS. Another example is the changing of documentation forms for emergency room facility charges. The time period for the next audit should be from the date of implementation, which would also allow a comparison of the accuracy using the old versus the new forms.
- Amount of resources. If the amount of resources (hours or dollars) required to complete an audit is known in advance, the population can be chosen with that consideration. For example, if it is known that the resources will only allow three months of payment testing against contracts, a likely population size is three months of payments. The amount of resources needs to be established based on the size of the organization and historical risks related to the organization or healthcare sector. For example, large hospice organizations should dedicate more resources than should smaller hospice organizations or organizations that provide services in areas with lower potential for abuse.

Sampling from the population is the next consideration. One of the significant considerations in methodology is whether you intend (or specifically do not intend) the results to be extrapolated. For any type of extrapolation, the sampling would be random, using some type of program. For example, RAT-STATs is the random selection and results testing published by the OIG. The sample selection could also be based upon the professional judgment of the auditor as to where potential issues may exist. If a random selection is not desired, a methodical selection process (e.g., every fifth then third claim in a population) can be used.

Legal Considerations

Unless mandated by a payer, there is no requirement that the audit population be statistically significant. Therefore, unless a statistically significant population is required, statistically significant audits should usually not be performed. You will need to work with your legal counsel when determining when to use a statistically valid sample and when not to use such a sample.

For outlier audits, the population data would be analyzed against the benchmark or other ranking. For example, the OIG published an audit report showing the percentage of long-term acute care hospital (LTCH) short-stay outliers in various categories aggregated for all LTCHs across the country. The auditor could collect a population of the hospital's data for the same period and compare it to the published OIG report to determine whether the hospital's specific patterns differ from those of hospitals across the country. If the patterns differ significantly, the auditor may choose to target a certain group of discharges for further review of accuracy and medical necessity (e.g., all orthopedic outliers if orthopedic admissions are the largest source of outlier patients).

Data Collection and Analysis for Different Audit Types

Billing and coding

When you access the downloadable material provided by this book, you will find a sample data collection tool for an outpatient Current Procedure Terminology (CPT®) coding audit (DataColl). The example uses paid claims as the sample unit. Each CPT line item from the selected claims would have each of the fields filled in on a spreadsheet. The sample demonstrates items that are downloaded from the system, which boxes are filled in by the auditor, the calculations based upon the explanation of benefits from the payer, an internally calculated amount (to check the payer accuracy), and the calculated amount after any errors are taken into account. Each of these data element types is color-coded. Although it will not contribute to an error calculation, it is an example of the additional types of elements that the auditor may want to review to determine whether policy is being followed.

Error rates for this type of audit could be reported as payment errors ([original payment – audited payment]/original payment), line-item errors (line items changed/total line items audited), or claims errors (claims with payment changes/total line items audited). For the payment errors in this type of audit, the organization may report overpayments separate from underpayments or may net (i.e., combine) the payment errors. In these types of billing and coding audits, corporate integrity agreements (CIA) published by the OIG generally allow a 5% overpayment error rate. If the error exceeds 5%, CIAs generally require additional testing and extrapolation, which could result in statistically valid reviews.

Although a claims error rate can be reported, such as reporting that issues were identified in 50% of claims reviewed, a net financial impact may be preferred. For example, one might report a net $1,000 overpayment from a universe of $100,000 reimbursement resulting in a 1% net overpayment error rate ($1,000/$100,000 = 0.01). This net overpayment of $1,000 could have identified a $5,000 overpayment and a $4,000 underpayment ($5,000 – $4,000 = $1,000). Sometimes it is a better practice to report results using the error rate based upon reimbursement as opposed to the percentage of claims reviewed where errors were identified.

When making any type of repayment to a payer, the focus should be on the error rate by reimbursement received, calculated both as a net dollar amount and as a net percentage based upon the reimbursement received. When making such repayments, the underpayments as well as any overpayments are typically reported.

Contract policy

Figure 10.1 shows an example of an audit for a medical director contract. In this case, the auditing standard is the policy, and there are notations about effective dates. Particularly for arrangements that have been in place for a period of time, the policy that is in effect when the arrangement is commenced may govern certain elements—for example, the approvals that are required for contract execution, or the documentation that is required as part of the file in the legal department.

FIGURE 10.1

Compliance Audit Department Contracting for Medical Director Services

SECTION A - GENERAL INFORMATION:	
Sample number:	
Medical director name:	
Hospital number:	
Hospital name:	
Original, renewal, or amended contract?	
Last commencement date (original or amended date):	Commenced after policy first effective? __ Yes __ No
Policy number in effect at the date of agreement:	
Term:	
Contractual payment:	
Estimate of time/hours for duties to be performed:	

FIGURE 10.1 (CONT.)		
SECTION B - CONTRACT STRUCTURE AND APPROVAL	Yes/No	Comments
1. Was supporting documentation submitted with the contract term sheet, including:	__ Check if section is not applicable because the contract commenced prior to the effective date of the policy or is an Auto Renewal Contract Term Sheet	
a. Documentation of duties to be performed		
b. Documentation of the hours to be worked		
c. Documentation of and signature upon the FMV calculations		
d. Medical Director Agreement, Record Certification, and Business Approvals		
e. A list of other physician directors at the hospital and their hours and compensation		
f. Copy of the contract to be reviewed (if not drafted by legal) or current contract if an amendment		
2. Was the Contract Term Sheet appropriately approved by the:	__ Check if section is not applicable because the contract commenced prior to the effective date of the policy or is an Auto Renewal Contract Term Sheet	
a. SVP?		
b. CEO of the hospital?		
c. Compliance department?		
3. Is there a fully executed contract, including:		
a. A list of duties to be performed by the director?		
b. The physician's and SVP's signature?		
c. A term of not less than one year?		
d. A rate consistent with the rate approved per the contract term sheet?		

FIGURE 10.1 (CONT.)

SECTION C- PAYMENTS						Yes/No	Comments
1. Are the medical director payments in accordance with the terms of the contract? (see Payment Calculation items a–e below)							
Payment Calculation - Medical Director							
Month (period ending)	a. Compensation paid	b. Hours reported	c. Contract rate	d. Compensation due	e. Difference	f. Was time sheet included?	g. Was time sheet signed by CEO and physician?
Month 1				$0.00	$0.00		
Month 2				$0.00	$0.00		
Month 3				$0.00	$0.00		
Month 4				$0.00	$0.00		
Month 5				$0.00	$0.00		
Month 6				$0.00	$0.00		
Month 7				$0.00	$0.00		
Month 8				$0.00	$0.00		
Month 9				$0.00	$0.00		
Month 10				$0.00	$0.00		
Month 11				$0.00	$0.00		
Month 12				$0.00	$0.00		
Total hours worked during the period: 0.00							
Average hours worked per month: 0.00							

SECTION D - SERVICE LOGS/ DOCUMENTATION OF PERFORMANCE	Yes/No	Comments
1. Is documentation available in the form of time sheets and/or other records demonstrating that all required duties have been performed in accordance with the terms of the contract?		See Payment Calculation, Section C, item f.
2. Is time sheet or other time reporting records signed by the CEO and physician?		See Payment Calculation, Section C, item g.
3. Was the "Medical Director for IRF Form" completed monthly by the physician?		Applicable only if the medical director is an IRF full-time medical director.

FIGURE 10.1 (CONT.)

SECTION E - OPERATIONAL TESTING	Yes/No	Comments
1. Is there a fully executed Business Associate Agreement signed by the CEO and physician?		
2. Is there evidence of completion of CIA requirements for the director? (This is a requirement for all medical directors and any program directors who work more than 160 hours per year. Should be completed within 30 days of the director's start date.)		
FINAL REPORTING QUESTIONS	Yes/No	Comments
1. Each arrangement was structured and approved in compliance with organization policies in effect at the start or renewal of the arrangement, including documentation of FMV.		See Section B
2. All payments for the most recent twelve (12)-month period have been made or received in accordance with the terms of the arrangement.		See Section C
3. Any required service logs or other documentation of performance of required duties has been completed in compliance with the terms of the arrangement and applicable policies.		See Section D

Many of the questions in this audit are based upon the organization's specific policy requirements. As an example, consider the fair market value of the compensation in the contract. Some organizations may require an outside valuation to be performed for each contract; other organizations may require valuations only for contracts above a certain overall threshold or above certain hourly rates that depend upon the type of service or specialty of the contracted provider (e.g., compensation over the 75th percentile of an applicable benchmarking entity, like Sullivan Cotter or the Medical Group Management Association).

Another difference may be the personnel that are required for approval. In some organizations, the compliance officer may approve each contract with a referral source. In others, he or she may not be involved at all in the approval process. As the scope of the audit is considered, the organization may decide not to test the approval portion at all, instead only looking at the payments and whether they match the terms of the executed contract.

Audit Report Outline

Objectives and methodology

The following is a sample report outline with the content to be covered in each section:

- Why is the audit being performed? Is it as a risk mitigation measure or because abnormal findings have been identified by an outside entity?
- Background—An overview of the law, regulation, or policy that is the subject of the audit.
- Objective—An overview of the testing performed. Why it is important to the organization? Is the purpose of the audit to test potential isolated or systemic issues?
- Review methodology:
    - Sampling unit—The unique item that is to be selected. This could be a paid claim (e.g., outpatient therapy claim for one month of services), a line item from a particular claim (e.g., cardiac catheterization services), etc.
    - Population—The population from which the sample items are selected.
    - Sample selection methodology—RAT-STAT random, targeted, judgmental, or other method (e.g., every fifth then third claim in a population).
- Review process—List of steps taken with each sample for the review.
- Review results—Results of the sample testing.
- Corrective action—Corrective action taken by the organization.
- Recommendations—Overall recommendations, which may include changes in policy or additional controls.
- Credentials—Credentials of the personnel who performed the audit.

Audit Life Cycle Tips

The following tips may help your audit organization operate more efficiently and avoid some common pitfalls:

- Planning. At the start of any audit, even those that have been performed previously, the audit team should go over background materials such as regulation and policy, the audit testing plan, and timing. During this process, it is essential to determine the scope of the audit, including such things as the following:
  - Items to be tested
  - Where the information is coming from
  - The time frame for the population
  - Deadlines for items such as population data download, sample selection, requests for detail data, and report findings
- Establishing criteria. Establish criteria to be used by each reviewer or for each unit in the sample to ensure consistency in findings.
- Reviewing. During this portion, it is critical to stick to the scope of the audit. If other items of interest are noted, they can be set aside for additional review outside the scope of the current audit. Enter findings into the audit form or database as the audit is conducted, as recollection from notes may not be sufficient to recall the issues identified.
- Determining findings/exceptions. If exceptions are found during the review, communicate with the auditing team, compliance officer, and legal counsel to determine whether there is any additional supporting documentation related to the potential exceptions found. It is better to hear counterarguments at this point rather than when findings are being presented to senior management.
- Report writing. Often, the more quickly the report writing is done after testing, the easier it is to complete.
- Expansion audits. If serious or systemic issues are found, an expanded audit may need to be performed. Take extra care with the planning process to determine factors such as whether an attorney should be involved, potential time periods for reviews, standard for reviewing (law versus policy), etc.

Monitoring Tools

Monitoring the chosen risk topics for the audit plan can be done in different ways. The frequency and length of monitoring may depend upon the level of risk.

Monitoring may be used to confirm adherence to policy. For example, if policy states that overall credit balances for the organization should be less than one day's reimbursement outstanding, monitoring can check for adherence to the organization's policy. Refinement of the monitoring may involve tracking more discrete elements. Using the credit balance scenario, monitoring by payer, service line, or responsible biller are examples of possible refinements.

Organizations may choose to also monitor implementation of new policies or controls. As an example, consider the following: A new charging methodology, based on objective data, was developed for a clinic. Multiple levels for services were necessary as described by the billing codes. Considering the general acuity of the clinic's patient population (this differs for an internal medicine practice versus a specialized area of medicine in which the percentage of healthy patients receiving preventive care is lower), the assignment of levels may be distributed on a curve. Monthly review of the number of claims billed to each level by practitioner may be performed for several months to ensure that the new methodology resulted in the desired effect.

At the conclusion of any auditing process, any errors or issues identified should be corrected with monitoring to ensure that any changes have been implemented effectively to decrease the potential of similar errors occurring in the future. By way of example, if a home health agency reviewed its medical records for the existence of a physician's certification for homebound status and found gaps, the home health agency should adopt a monitoring program to ensure that such homebound status certification is received for each patient. An example of effective monitoring for such an issue would include designating one person as responsible for reviewing each medical record at designated times to ensure that the appropriate physician certification of homebound status is included based upon the entities' policy and all applicable rules and regulations.

Monitoring and auditing can help the compliance department determine whether the overall compliance program is operating as intended. Monitoring also helps to verify whether the controls, such as training, are effective. Demonstrating an effective auditing program through monitoring will assist in mitigating overall compliance risk for the organization.

The auditing and monitoring activities should also be periodically reported to the board. A best practice is to report such activities at least twice a year to the board in a duly-called meeting. Because the auditing and monitoring activities are indicators of an effective compliance program, the board should be assured of the existence and results of these activities.

Chapter 11

Effective Internal Investigations

The day will come when a hotline call, a routine claims review, or a whistleblower's complaint brings a compliance concern or some bad news from the compliance front. An employee or competitor may suggest that someone within your organization has engaged in criminal or civil acts or omissions. If these events occur, you must ask the following questions: Is the whistleblower correct? What is the possibility that the issue identified is true? Has the auditor unearthed a previously unrecognized problem? The answers to these questions may cause you to decide whether to undertake an internal investigation.

It is important to note that this chapter concerns internal investigations. Internal investigations can run the gamut from a simple review of a discrete potential compliance issue (e.g., medical report given to wrong patient) up to and including an alleged criminal violation, such as a violation of the Anti-Kickback Statute (e.g., above fair market value compensation to a group of employed neurosurgeons). Regardless of the issue being reported, and regardless of the source, it is important that the compliance officer ensure that a thorough investigation/review is conducted to determine whether any reported allegation is substantiated. As you will learn in this chapter, the scope of the investigation will depend upon the issue being reported. Although this chapter primarily deals with major investigations, the same steps should be considered by the compliance officer related to any compliance issue. Although all reported issues should be investigated, even issues that are brought to the attention of the organization through an anonymous hotline report, investigations concerning greater potential liability, including large repayments, warrant heightened consideration and safeguards.

In many companies, the compliance officer is the first to become aware of a potential compliance problem that could lead to civil or criminal liability or even a simple repayment or reprocessing of claims. A best practice is to give the compliance officer the authority to conduct internal investigations. If this is not the case, however, it is likely that the board of directors or other governing committee will have the ultimate authority to make that decision.

One of the primary tasks for the compliance officer, therefore, is to provide the decision-maker with enough information to make a reasonable and rational decision about the scope and conduct of an internal investigation. Because of potential negative investigation results, it is important for compliance officers to be able to report directly to the board on important matters. The inability to do so can negatively impact the board's response to alleged noncompliant conduct.

Before the Investigation Begins

Unless the compliance officer has the independent and unfettered right to initiate and conduct an investigation, the initial task of the compliance officer will be to advise the decision-makers about the nature of the potential noncompliant behavior and to enable them to make the appropriate decision. The officer should be careful not to sensationalize or personalize the known facts or to speculate about the outcomes or consequences before the investigation begins.

Because all the facts will not be known, the compliance officer may be in the uncomfortable position of repeating allegations or assertions made by someone perceived as "not on the same side" as the provider, giving rise to skepticism. That skepticism leads naturally to a discussion of the benefits of further information gathering. Some individuals may elect to forgo an investigation if the person reporting it is viewed as a "troublemaker"—this is a bad decision, with potentially harmful consequences. By engaging in a formal internal investigation, the provider must not speculate about the scope of real or suspected problems, nor should it rely on rumors, supposition, or appearances. If no problem is revealed, the provider may be able to defuse a volatile situation with a potential whistleblower or a government investigator.

Before conducting an internal investigation, it is critically important to plan and outline its structure. The plan should include what documents will be reviewed, what financial statements need to be obtained, which employees will be interviewed, and what other ancillary information is needed (e.g., prior legal advice, prior audit results or monitoring activities, fair market value documentation, coding and billing instructions). The outline should be in writing and shared with key organizational decision-makers, including the compliance committee. Obviously, as the investigation proceeds, the tasks involved may need to be modified as information is gathered.

If there truly is a problem, the investigation should unearth illegal, improper, or reckless conduct. Once the facts are known, the provider can undertake appropriate remedial actions to ensure that mistakes are not ongoing or repeated. Also, the provider can determine whether remedial action, including repayment of reimbursement or self-reports to governmental agencies or contractors, should be implemented.

Triggers for an Internal Investigation

Historically, many companies initiated internal investigations only upon learning that they were the subjects of a government probe. However, in today's current enforcement environment, such laxity is unlikely to be tolerated by government prosecutors. For-profit healthcare organizations must be vigilant in conducting internal investigations regarding alleged misconduct, primarily due to the requirements under the Sarbanes-Oxley Act and also derivative shareholder lawsuits. However, nonprofit healthcare organizations are not immune to internal misconduct and must also be aggressive in initiating internal investigations to detect and prevent wrongdoing.

Due to the complexity of healthcare regulations, including reimbursement regulations and the strict requirements around financial arrangements with referral sources, including physicians, internal investigations are extremely common. If organizations do not conduct internal investigations, it is possible that they do not have effective compliance programs in place. Effective compliance programs identify potential misconduct and, upon identification, undertake internal investigations.

As part of an effective compliance program, your organization should be promoting an open reporting process so that any and all potential misconduct can be reported and investigated. Your organization will save a lot of money and time if issues are reported internally and appropriately investigated as opposed to being subject to a governmental inquiry. The only way issues can be reported and investigated is by establishing an open and nonretaliatory reporting process. When issues are reported, they must be reviewed and investigated.

A healthcare entity may receive allegations of corporate wrongdoing from several different sources: employees, customers, competitors, auditors, whistleblowers, or the government. Common sense and good business judgment usually dictate the initiation of an internal investigation in situations where a problem appears to exist and may serve as the basis for civil or criminal liability, even if no third parties or governmental entities are involved. Conducting an investigation in these circumstances is not only in the entity's self-interest but also provides an opportunity to be proactive, rather than defensive or reactive. Also, in a self-initiated review, the entity controls the review's flow and resource allocation instead of having these things dictated by the government, payer, or *qui tam* relator.

Further, the government may decline prosecution of an entity that can demonstrate its intolerance of corporate wrongdoing through an effective corporate compliance program, the appropriate investigatory responses to allegations of misconduct, and appropriate disciplinary and remedial measures. Even if the entity is prosecuted and found guilty, its demonstrated commitment to compliance and being a good corporate citizen can result in significant mitigation of a potential criminal fine under the U.S. Sentencing Guidelines.

In this chapter, we will discuss the different triggers for internal investigations. In each of these situations, a healthcare entity must gather the applicable facts to develop an appropriate response and to justify its subsequent actions, including whether to initiate a full internal investigation, hire outside experts, or consider the matter closed.

Employee Complaints

Employees are often the greatest source of "tips" regarding compliance issues. A problem could come to light through an entity's normal lines of reporting, an exit interview, the compliance officer, or an anonymous call to the entity's hotline. However, not all employee complaints warrant a full-blown, detailed internal investigation. Although all reported issues should be investigated, the compliance officer needs to be able to sift through employee complaints to determine which ones warrant a more comprehensive review. Thus, the compliance officer should triage reported issues and dedicate resources based upon the type of issue being reported and source of the reports (e.g., suspected *qui tam* relator).

As stated previously, promote your organization's reporting process to your employees. Employees should be encouraged to bring potential compliance issues to the attention of their supervisors, senior executives, or the compliance officer; they may also make a report through your organization's anonymous hotline. You will need to promote your nonretaliation policy and emphasize this policy to every employee who reports a compliance concern. Employees will know that your compliance program takes compliance issues seriously if they witness you performing internal investigations and closing each investigation with appropriate corrective action. Further, if the identity of the employee who brought the concern to the attention of the organization is known, the closure of the investigation should be communicated to that employee. If your employees see that issues are being investigated and that appropriate corrective action is taken, they will believe that the organization has an effective compliance program and will be more willing to bring issues to the organization's attention, as opposed to either not reporting at all or choosing to bring the issues to the government.

Internal Audits and Surveys

Healthcare companies should actively self-monitor for noncompliant activity. Periodic audits or reviews may reveal omissions or discrepancies that could result in civil or criminal liability. Any discrepancy that is an overpayment must be repaid within 60 days of the determination of the overpayment, which means within 60 days after the overpayment has been quantified after using reasonable due diligence and resources. If the audits or reviews are conducted pursuant to a court-mandated compliance program or corporate integrity agreement (CIA), the entity may be required to self-disclose the problem within a sooner time frame based upon the terms of the mandated program.

Companies must resist the temptation to believe that the anomalies or inconsistencies uncovered by an internal audit or survey are inconsequential and will never become public. Rather, an internal investigation should be conducted to determine the magnitude of the problem if the internal audit or survey findings suggest potential wrongdoing. An internal investigation can then clarify whether the entity is a victim of employee wrongdoing or possibly responsible for the unlawful conduct or conduct inconsistent with government rules or regulations. A sign of an effective compliance program is the presence of an active audit program and repayment to Medicare, Medicaid, third-party payers, and patients. A history of no repayments may be due to an ineffective compliance program.

Civil Suits and *Qui Tam* Relator Actions

Some companies first learn of possible corporate wrongdoing only after being served with a civil complaint by a third party, such as a former employee, a supplier, or a competitor. The existence of a private lawsuit, such as a contract dispute or tort action, strongly favors the commencement of an internal investigation. Such an investigation will help predict the development of the plaintiff's case, identify weaknesses in that case, and uncover impeaching material against potentially adverse witnesses.

The False Claims Act (FCA), 31 USC §§3729–33, contains provisions that allow employees, competitors, and third parties to bring suits on behalf of the government as *qui tam* relators or whistleblowers. Even an employee who committed the acts that formed the basis for a *qui tam* action can be the *qui tam* relator. The government has the option to intervene and assume control of the case, or the relator may pursue the matter if the government elects not to intervene. Courts generally view *qui tam* cases in which the government declined to intervene with skepticism. Any judgment or settlement brought in by a *qui tam* litigant is a judgment or settlement with the government, with the *qui tam* litigant receiving 15%–25% of the judgment/settlement.

Government audits, reports, inspections, and inquiries may reveal questionable business practices of a business unit or a group of employees. In those circumstances, the entity should initiate an internal investigation to determine the scope and seriousness of the alleged problematic conduct. Once the facts are known, the entity can develop the most appropriate strategy for dealing with the government. If the questionable conduct came to light via a government audit, report, inspection, or inquiry, the entity will have to be prepared, through an internal investigation, to respond to the government.

Subpoenas and Search Warrants

A healthcare entity may learn of allegations of wrongdoing only after employees are approached by federal investigators or after being served with an administrative or grand jury subpoena—or, in the worst-case scenario, the execution of a search warrant. If the government has chosen this route, the prosecutor generally believes that some very serious violation has occurred, and a criminal prosecution is likely to happen. Experienced healthcare legal counsel should be contacted immediately to guide the organization in responding to the subpoena or search warrant. In these situations, an entity has no choice but to conduct an internal investigation. The investigation should, at a minimum, mirror the government's investigation.

The information gathered from the internal investigation can provide senior management with a realistic understanding of the entity's civil or criminal exposure and an appreciation of the government's view of the case. This knowledge will place the entity in a better position when negotiating with the government and may support the entity's contention that the unlawful conduct was an aberration that was missed by an otherwise effective compliance program.

Preserving Attorney-Client Privilege and Work-Product Protection

Successful internal investigations require a great deal of planning, skill, and diplomacy. Depending on the nature of the alleged misconduct, especially if criminal conduct is alleged, healthcare companies should consider conducting investigations in a manner that scrupulously maintains the protections afforded by attorney-client privilege and work-product protection.

If attorney-client privileges are to be preserved, the investigation should be conducted under the direction of an attorney experienced in and knowledgeable of the healthcare industry and the issues alleged. By way of example, if the allegation concerns financial relationships with referring physicians, the organization should engage an attorney with significant experience in the intricacies of the Stark Law and Anti-Kickback Statute. The attorney should also conduct the investigation in a way that minimizes the potential hazards that may arise.

Corporations conducting internal investigations face two overriding needs: the need to obtain accurate information promptly and respond to it appropriately and the need to maintain the confidentiality of the investigation and protect acquired information from undesired disclosure.

Privilege issues often present thorny problems for companies conducting internal investigations. Employee interviews, the selection and review of investigation-related documents, the preparation of legal and factual memoranda, and the final investigation report all potentially implicate attorney-client privilege, work-product protection, and self-evaluative privilege. These protections should be guarded jealously, as decisions that implicate them can have a dramatic effect upon the ultimate outcome of an internal investigation.

FIGURE 11.1

What Is Attorney-Client Privilege?

Attorney-client privilege provides protection for a limited class of communications. It provides that all communications between an attorney and client that are made for the purpose of obtaining or giving legal advice are confidential. The privilege does not, however, protect the underlying preexisting facts from disclosure. Of course, many government investigations request, in exchange for leniency of penalties, that attorney-client documents be opened for review.

The application of attorney-client privilege is somewhat more complicated in situations where the client is a corporation. Although corporations are entitled to the same protection of confidentiality as noncorporate clients, the application of the privilege often relies on which corporate officials and employees sufficiently personify the corporation as a client.

In order to protect attorney-client privilege, those involved in the investigation need to understand that only communications with the attorney seeking legal advice are privileged. Therefore, employees should be advised in all communications to report only the facts and not necessarily draw conclusions from the facts. Ideally, the communications to and from the attorney should be marked as "privileged and confidential attorney-client communication." Employees need to be warned that any type of communication that is made outside of correspondences to and from an attorney seeking legal advice could be freely discovered, as such communications may not be protected under attorney-client privilege. Further, if some analysis is communicated outside of the context of attorney-client privilege, all information related to the nonconfidential communication can be freely discovered by the government and opposing parties, such as litigants.

All parties also need to know and understand that attorney-client privilege is held by the client. Therefore, the client can waive this privilege. Because the privilege is held by the client, attorneys also need to be vigilant about what is communicated, especially if the communication is in writing or via email.

FIGURE 11.2
What Is Work-Product Protection?
Work-product protection provides immunity to a broad class of communications and documents prepared in anticipation of litigation. Its purpose is to provide a lawyer with a certain degree of privacy and freedom from unnecessary intrusion by opposing parties and their counsel. In contrast to attorney-client privilege, which protects only communications, work-product protection is commonly asserted to preserve the confidentiality of an attorney's mental impressions, conclusions, opinions, or legal theories. This protection also differs from attorney-client privilege in that both the client and the lawyer hold it. Work-product protection covers only those materials prepared in "anticipation of litigation," not those prepared for other business purposes, such as public relations or financial auditing. Although collateral use of internal investigation results may muddy the already murky waters of the privilege, courts have been willing to consider materials generated during an internal investigation as predicates to litigation, even if litigation does not occur. Therefore, most work product generated by the attorney during an investigation should be protected through work-product privilege.

Conducting Employee Interviews

Interviewing employees is one of the most dependable ways to determine facts in an internal investigation. Employees can supply investigators not only with most of the relevant facts at issue but also with the context and rationale for many otherwise questionable practices. However, note that such interviews need to be handled sensitively to minimize the possibility of internal personnel conflicts or the waiving of attorney-client privilege and work-product protection.

Employee interviews must be handled with careful planning and execution. The interviewer must be able to establish a rapport with the employee quickly and must ask questions that do not make the employee defensive. He or she must be able to draw out as much relevant information as the employee possesses.

Structuring interviews

Investigators must structure employee interviews with the following four goals in mind:

1. Obtaining truthful information
2. Preserving confidentiality
3. Fulfilling ethical obligations
4. Minimizing the interviewer's and the entity's criminal and legal exposure during the investigation process

These goals can all be realized if the interviewer instructs the employee prior to conducting the interview about the interviewer's role and the employee's responsibilities. If an attorney conducts the interview, the attorney must inform the employee that he or she represents the organization, not the employee.

All matters discussed in the interview can be shared with the organization's executives involved in the investigation.

The employee's participation in the investigation, including interviews, can be a condition of continued employment. If an employee refuses to participate in the investigation or does not participate in good faith, the employee may be terminated. However, organizations should use caution to ensure that such termination cannot be perceived as retaliation, especially if the employee was the original source of the allegation.

Employees do not have the right to have their attorney present during interviews; however, they do have the right to consult with their own legal counsel. Also, if the employee is covered by a labor contract, upon employee request, a coworker can accompany the employee during the interview.

Interviews should be carefully orchestrated. The interviewer should establish a road map and outline of the issues to be covered. Ideally, most questions posed during the interview process should be open-ended, permitting the employee to elaborate regarding the facts and information that he or she knows. The interviewer must also be very clear as to whether the employee is stating facts, opinion, or speculation based upon hearsay from others in the organization.

The interviewer must also understand how the employee became aware of any facts asserted during the interview. He or she may request documents from the employee and may need to conduct follow-up interviews with the employee based upon this additional documentation, as well as interviews with other employees within the organization.

Lastly, interviewers should expect that employees may be extremely nervous or defensive during an interview. It is up to the interviewer to make the employee as comfortable as possible. Conducting employee interviews is not an easy job; thus, selecting effective interviewers is extremely important for an effective internal investigation.

Avoiding Civil Liability

Hasty, incomplete, or improperly conducted employee interviews can substantially increase a healthcare entity's liability. Employees who feel wrongly accused or maligned by a workplace interview have legal weapons against their employer, even if they are not disciplined as a result of the interview. These legal challenges usually use one of a handful of tort theories: intentional infliction of emotional distress, invasion of privacy, defamation, or false imprisonment.

Employee interviews conducted in a generally reasonable manner normally do not result in liability. Nevertheless, companies should be mindful about how they handle employee interviews because courts, when reviewing employee tort claims, will take into consideration the length of the interview, the employer's conduct during the interview, whether the employer had a good-faith belief that the interviewed employee had information that was useful in the investigation, and whether the employer had a good-faith belief that the employee had engaged in improper conduct or was involved in the alleged conduct.

Disclosure of Overpayments

If the internal investigation identifies areas of concern, the provider should undertake remedial steps to ensure that any compliance issues are resolved going forward. Such steps may involve additional training of employees and staff members, preparation or amendment of policies and procedures, institution of checks and cross-checks, issuance of reprimands, or termination of malfeasant employees.

The provider may decide to limit its response to those internal compliance efforts and take no further action, assuming that it is not under any legal obligation to disclose its findings. But even if the law does not expressly obligate a provider to disclose its findings, good compliance practice dictates that the provider should at least consider whether the results of an internal investigation should be disclosed to a carrier, a Medicare Administrative Contractor (MAC), a governmental agency, or even a private payer. This disclosure should also consider the repayment of inappropriately paid claims, if applicable.

Is a provider required to disclose the results of its investigation voluntarily?

When properly protected under attorney-client privilege, the results of some internal investigations do not have to be disclosed. Absent a specific duty to disclose, corporations are not legally required to report past wrongdoing to the government. However, where the internal investigation uncovers an overpayment, there is an obligation to repay the overpayment.

In 2010, the FCA was substantially modified to require, among other actions, that overpayments be repaid within 60 days of determining the overpayment. Some thought that the 60-day period commenced upon the discovery of a potential overpayment, but the statute was later clarified to state that the 60-day repayment period actually commences upon determination of the overpayment. "Determination" has been interpreted to mean after the ability to quantify the amount of the overpayment.

These requirements mean that the healthcare entity has to commit sufficient resources and due diligence to determine the amount of the overpayment. Once the amount of the overpayment has been quantified, the 60-day period commences. If a provider wanted to be conservative and not rely on the quantification process to end to commence the 60-day repayment period, the provider may notify the payer, such as the MAC, that a potential overpayment has been discovered with assurance that the organization will commit sufficient resources to quantify the amount of the overpayment. If notice is provided to the MAC that an issue is being investigated, the MAC may accept the notice as being compliant with the 60-day period even though the quantification report to the MAC will be more than 60 days from the discovery of the issue. Notice to the payer prior to the end of the quantification process should be considered if the quantification process is expected to take a long time. Legal counsel should be consulted regarding using the notice to the payer strategy prior to the completion of the quantification process.

The changes to the FCA also created what many refer to as a "reverse false claim." A reverse false claim occurs when the organization identifies an overpayment but knowingly decides to keep the overpayment and not repay the government. By so doing, the organization is committing a violation under the FCA.

Further, the changes to the FCA incorporated a coconspirator provision under which any person involved with knowingly submitting a false claim or intentionally keeping an overpayment can be personally liable under the FCA.

An overpayment may be established when an organization identifies a Stark Law violation. By way of example, if the organization identifies a two-year period during which it had a financial arrangement with a referring physician that did not fully conform with a Stark Law exception, all of the referrals of Medicare patients by the tainted physician are subject to repayment.

Just like a billing error, intentionally deciding to retain the reimbursement from referrals during a period when the physician and designated health service entity, such as a hospital or a laboratory, did not fully meet a Stark exception counts as an overpayment and is subject to the rules discussed above. Thus, if a known Stark violation has occurred and the reimbursement from the tainted physician's referrals is retained by the organization, the organization has committed a reverse false claim, and any person involved in the decision-making process to retain such reimbursement could be held responsible as a coconspirator under the FCA.

The reverse false claims liability under the FCA significantly changed how organizations are to respond to overpayments, whether they occur due to billing and documentation issues or Stark Law violations.

Determining "known" overpayments

Given the complexity of Medicare rules and regulations, there may be good-faith uncertainty over the appropriateness of certain claims and, thus, whether there is a known overpayment. Providers need to analyze the issues surrounding alleged overpayments to determine whether the amount received can be clearly determined to have been paid in error. Knowledge under the FCA is defined as actual knowledge, reckless disregard, or intentional indifference to the law. Thus, not auditing billing systems and protocol, or not reviewing financial arrangements for Stark Law compliance, can generate "known" overpayments due to the reckless disregard or intentional indifference standards under the FCA.

An internal investigation may reveal illegal behavior under the Anti-Kickback Statute (42 USC §1320a–7b). Prior to the 2010 modifications to the FCA, a majority of courts held that submission of claims that were based upon Anti-Kickback Statute violations were also deemed to be false claims. However, some courts and prosecutors did not automatically hold that claims submitted as a result of referrals derived through illegal kickback schemes were false claims. In 2010, as part of the Patient Protection and Affordable Care Act, the FCA was modified to include, as false claims, claims submitted that were received in violation of the Anti-Kickback Statute. This change to the FCA also held that "a person need not have actual knowledge ... or specific intent to commit a violation" of the Anti-Kickback Statute. Thus, the government can bring false claims actions against providers who violate the statute.

Voluntary disclosure of overpayments may be required under the terms of an existing CIA. Most settlements under the FCA, or with the Office of Inspector General (OIG) alone, result in the provider agreeing to a CIA. The typical CIA requires a provider to put compliance measures in place to ensure the integrity of federal healthcare program claims submitted by the provider. Such measures generally include requirements to do the following:

- Hire a compliance officer and appoint a compliance committee
- Develop written standards and policies
- Conduct an effective employee training program
- Audit billings to federal healthcare programs
- Establish a hotline
- Restrict employment of excluded individuals
- Submit various reports to the OIG, including annual reports about the provider's compliance activities

Most significantly, guidance on CIAs makes clear that the CIA imposes express obligations on providers to report overpayments. The risk of failing to comply with the CIA is that the settlement agreement will be violated, and the provider may once again be subject to prosecution for the claims settled and possible exclusion from the Medicare program.

Even if your organization does not have a CIA with the OIG, many of the general requirements under CIAs can guide you in the development, implementation, and oversight of your compliance program. This is especially true for CIAs specific to your industry sector (e.g., hospitals, laboratories, pharmaceutical companies, device manufacturers).

Advantages and Disadvantages of Voluntary Disclosure

When voluntary disclosure is an option rather than an obligation, the provider may encounter diverse opinions among its decision-makers. Some may express a desire to bring the potential problem to the attention of the government and attempt to resolve the matter quickly without incurring criminal penalties, civil fines, or exclusions. On the other hand, some decision-makers might prefer not to draw the scrutiny of an enforcement agency, reasoning that the risks of that scrutiny outweigh its potential positives. Deciding whether to disclose an issue requires a complex analysis of all the facts and circumstances, as well as a balancing of the benefits and risks. Consultation with experienced healthcare legal counsel is strongly advised to understand what issues are required to be reported, how to quantify the amount of the overpayment, and how to report the issue.

Advantages of voluntary disclosure

Following is a discussion of some advantages of voluntary disclosure.

The provider controls the message

Self-disclosure involves providing a narrative that will identify the overpayment and possible explanation of the error that caused it. To disclose problems voluntarily, the provider should draft a document that accurately states the events surrounding the noncompliant issue, how the issue was discovered, and what safeguards the provider has put in place to prevent such irregularity in the future.

If the law is vague, the provider can highlight the legal ambiguity and describe alternative interpretations. The narrative should avoid legal conclusions (such as that the claims were "false" or that the billing agent "knew" that the claims were wrong) and admissions against its interest. The provider should highlight the importance of the compliance program within the institution, especially if the issue was discovered as a result of the organization's compliance initiatives.

Further inquiry and enforcement are limited

By voluntarily disclosing the mistake, the provider may persuade the government to forgo any enforcement actions beyond repayment. This is especially true where appropriate compliance efforts have been undertaken (e.g., remedial training, dismissal of the wrongdoers, establishment of new control mechanisms, or compliance with OIG Model Compliance Program elements).

The organization has a better chance of avoiding a CIA

By bringing the problem to the OIG's attention, the provider may earn considerable credibility. The OIG may rely upon the organization's investigative report in verifying the disclosed information and reporting the matter. Voluntary disclosure may thereby prevent a disruptive outside investigation and expensive and time-consuming litigation by the enforcement agency. If an outside inquiry cannot be avoided entirely, the disclosure may either avoid or allow negotiation of the scope of the government's investigation and employee interviews. It may also enable the provider to avoid discovery battles.

In the event that the government goes forward with an enforcement action based on the voluntary disclosure, the disclosing party may nonetheless receive more favorable treatment. For example, a CIA may not be required if a matter is settled based on a self-disclosure. In its November 20, 2001, "Open Letter to Health Care Providers," the OIG modified the policies applicable in civil settlement processes, including CIAs:

> *We also recognize that in certain cases it may be appropriate to release the OIG's administrative exclusion authorities without a corporate integrity agreement. I have directed my staff to consider the following criteria when determining whether to require a corporate integrity agreement, and, if so, the substance of that agreement: (1) whether the provider self-disclosed the alleged misconduct.*

Similarly, the OIG has published nonbinding guidelines to be used in assessing whether to impose the permissive exclusion on a provider. See "Criteria for Implementing Permissive Exclusion Authority Under Section 1128(b)(7) of the [SSA]," 62 FR 67, 392 (1997). These guidelines identify specific factors and explain how they would be used by the OIG to assess a permissive exclusion decision. The OIG's criteria include the general category of "Defendant's Response to Allegations/Determination of Unlawful Conduct" and asks the following within that category: Did the defendant bring the activity in question to the attention of the appropriate government officials prior to the government action (e.g., was there any voluntary disclosure regarding the alleged wrongful conduct)?

Fines and penalties may be reduced

In return for voluntary submission of information that documents wrongdoing, the provider may seek to resolve the improper billing issue by repaying the amount improperly paid. By saving the government the cost of investigation, the provider may incur only a smaller penalty compared to what the government could have sought had the settlement resulted from the government's own investigation.

The disclosure gives the provider a reasonable chance to mitigate fines and penalties. Under the FCA, 31 §3729, a disclosure will reduce exposure to fines. Instead of triple damages, the Department of Justice (DOJ) is limited to double damages.

Similarly, *U.S. Sentencing Commission Guidelines Manual* §5K2.16, Voluntary Disclosure of Offense (policy statement), provides that if the defendant voluntarily discloses to authorities the existence of, and accepts responsibility for, the offense prior to the discovery of such offense, "a departure below the applicable sentencing guideline range for that offense may be warranted."

According to the *U.S. Sentencing Commission Guidelines,* the DOJ will "presumptively consider" resolving reported issues through what is known as a "declination." A declination is when the DOJ closes the issues subject to the self-report without imposing a penalty and with no presumption of guilt or innocence. The presumption of declination will be considered by the DOJ only when aggravating circumstances related to the seriousness of the offense are not present. The DOJ provided a list of aggravating circumstances, which include involvement by executive management of the entity in the misconduct, a significant end profit to the entity from the misconduct, pervasiveness of the misconduct within the entity, and criminal recidivism. Standards for voluntary self-disclosure will be met if the organization discloses in the following ways:

1. Discloses before imminent threat of disclosure by a third-party or a government investigation
2. Discloses within a reasonably prompt time frame after discovering the offense
3. Report discloses all known relative facts
4. Reporting organization continuously reports relevant facts through further investigation after the submission of the disclosure

5. Proactively cooperates after the submission of the disclosure
6. Discloses of all relevant documents and information
7. Coordinates internal investigative steps with the DOJ
8. Officers and employees, and third-parties where possible (e.g., auditors, accountants, legal counsel [if attorney-client privilege is waived]), are made available to the DOJ for interviews

The voluntary disclosure through the *U.S. Sentencing Commission Guidelines* further require that the reporting entity makes "timely and appropriate remediation," which includes the following:

1. A thorough analysis of the underlying conduct and appropriate remediation taken
2. Implementation of an effective compliance and ethics program
3. Appropriate disciplinary action taken with employees and contractors
4. Retention of all business records applicable to self-report during pendency of resolution of the issues involved in the voluntary report
5. Appropriate additional steps to demonstrate the organization's recognition of the seriousness of the reported misconduct

As noted above, one of the key factors the DOJ will consider is whether the reporting organization has implemented an effective compliance program. As noted in the guidelines, and as further emphasized in this book, the DOJ will look at the effectiveness of the organization's compliance program based upon the size and sophistication of the reporting entity, culture of compliance within the organization, dedication of appropriate and sufficient resources to compliance activities, and evidence that designated compliance personnel, including the compliance officer, have appropriate and meaningful access to management, including the chief executive officer and the board.

The *U.S. Sentencing Commission Guidelines* is further evidence that the best insurance policy against possible fines and penalties by the government is an effective compliance program.

In addition, in determining the culpability score of an organization (and, therefore, the fine amount), the *U.S. Sentencing Commission Guidelines* provide a significant incentive to those organizations that self-report. If an organization self-reports "prior to an imminent threat of disclosure or government investigation" and "within a reasonably prompt time after becoming aware of the offense," the organization's culpability score can be reduced. Moreover, for an organization to get credit under the guidelines for having an effective compliance program, it must not "unreasonably delay" reporting the offense to the government.

Types of self-disclosure

If an overpayment has been identified, the provider can make the repayment to the MAC or the carrier. If the claims being repaid can be reprocessed (typically within 18 months of when the claim was paid), the provider can choose to simply reprocess the claim without conducting a formal repayment through written notice to the MAC or the carrier. If the affected claims are outside of the reprocessing period, the provider will need to send a formal repayment letter to the MAC or carrier explaining the issue that caused the overpayment, how it was discovered, how the organization quantified the amount of the overpayment, and the corrective actions and safeguards performed by the provider.

For Stark Law infractions, providers can use the Self-Referral Disclosure Protocol (SRDP). The process for making a Stark Law self-disclosure can be found at the Centers for Medicare & Medicaid Services (CMS) website at *www.cms.gov*. If the provider voluntarily reports a Stark Law violation and quantifies the reimbursement received from referrals from tainted physicians, CMS has the power to negotiate a settlement with the provider filing the self-report. For information regarding settlements that have occurred using the SRDP, with a brief explanation of the issue being settled and the amount of the settlement, see *www.cms.gov/medicare/fraud-and-abuse/physicianselfreferral/self-referral-disclosure-protocol-settlements.*

If the issue identified is a potential violation of the Anti-Kickback Statute or the Civil Monetary Penalties Statute, the provider can self-report using the OIG Self-Disclosure Protocol. Information regarding this protocol can be found on the OIG's website at *https://oig.hhs.gov/compliance/self-disclosure-info/index.asp.*

If a Stark Law violation potentially implicates the Anti-Kickback Statute or the Civil Monetary Penalties Statute, providers are to use the OIG Self-Disclosure Protocol instead of the SRDP.

For any potential self-disclosure, especially when using the SRDP and the OIG Self-Disclosure Protocol, consult legal counsel with significant experience in the healthcare industry and in pursuing self-disclosures.

Disadvantages of voluntary disclosure

Although the advantages of voluntary disclosure are measured against the assumption that the government will learn of the errors through sources other than self-disclosure, the disadvantages are measured against the assumption that, absent the disclosure, the matter will be disclosed by a third party (e.g., a MAC, carrier, or competitor) to an enforcement agency by a *qui tam* action.

The provider is not guaranteed to get a break

Given that no two noncompliant activities are the same, there is no guarantee that voluntary disclosure will result in a decision by the government to refrain from proceeding criminally or civilly against the provider. Although the provider might be credited to some extent for its compliance efforts, the provider could remain subject to potential liability based on its failure to prevent the illegal or inappropriate activity, especially if egregious behavior has occurred or if the organization has had previous issues of noncompliance with the government.

The provider may waive certain privileges

According to the *U.S. Sentencing Commission Guidelines,* one of the factors that the government can consider when determining fines and penalties is whether the provider waived attorney-client privilege and disclosed all of the information regarding the issue. As noted above, because the organization owns the attorney-client privilege, it is up to the provider to decide whether to waive that privilege. If the provider is going to use an "advice of legal counsel" defense, it will very likely have to waive its attorney-client privilege to show the government what type of legal advice it received related to the issue being reported.

Prior to waiving the privilege, the privileged documents should be carefully analyzed to make sure that they do not discuss or reveal other ancillary issues that are not related to the issue being reported. Again, it is advisable to consult legal counsel with experience in the healthcare arena in order to assess the benefits and risks of waiving attorney-client privilege.

Balancing the risks and benefits

The balancing of benefits and risks is complex and should be undertaken only with advice of knowledgeable counsel. If the best direction is not clear, answer the following questions to help inform the decision-making process:

- Can you handle the situation as an ordinary matter? If providers can withdraw or amend erroneous claims before adjudication by the MAC, they can "disclose" in that way, thereby potentially avoiding the additional expense and aggravation of having the claims considered to be disclosures.
- Are the circumstances and seriousness of the underlying misconduct such that a self-disclosure is likely to reduce the burden of an investigation and thereby mitigate any penalties?
- What is at stake? Is someone's personal freedom at risk because of a potential jail sentence? If a federal healthcare program financial loss has occurred, what was the extent of such loss? Is the provider willing to repay the overpayment? If not, can the provider seek to reduce the penalties based on its ability to repay?
- Has the provider had the same or similar problems with the OIG, CMS, the carrier, the MAC, or the state? Is there evidence that the provider knew, or should have known, that its conduct was prohibited?

- Is the provider willing to make the necessary changes in billing practices, standards of conduct, and internal control systems to ensure compliance with the law going forward?

When it comes to self-disclosure, there is no single right answer for every situation. However, by taking into account the risks and benefits outlined in the preceding pages, the provider, through discussion with competent healthcare legal counsel, can try to steer the best course and make the appropriate decision.

In conclusion, all reported issues should be investigated. Compliance officers should triage issues and dedicate resources depending on the potential liability/exposure to the organization. Serious potential exposure or liability should receive the highest degree of investigation, including the involvement of experienced healthcare legal counsel, when warranted. If mistakes or improper action have been substantiated, repayments or self-disclosures should be conducted.

Appendix

Important Compliance Terminology

The following are some important compliance terms with which you should become familiar.

TERM	DEFINITION
Accountable care organization (ACO)	A group of doctors, hospitals, and other healthcare providers that comes together voluntarily to give coordinated, high-quality care to its Medicare patients. Savings through an ACO can be shared with the ACO participants.
Administrative simplification	Title II, Subtitle F of HIPAA, which authorizes the U.S. Department of Health and Human Services (HHS) to adopt standards for transactions and code sets that are used to exchange health data; adopt standard identifiers for health plans, healthcare providers, employers, and individuals for use on standard transactions; and adopt standards to protect the security and privacy of personally identifiable health information.
Admitting diagnosis code	A code indicating a patient's diagnosis at admission.
Advance beneficiary notice	A notice that a doctor or supplier should give a Medicare beneficiary to sign when the doctor or supplier provides a service that he or she believes Medicare will not pay for or consider medically necessary. Even though Medicare may not cover the service, the treating physician may still believe that the patient needs it.
Affordable Care Act (ACA)	A federal law adopted in March 2010 as part of President Obama's healthcare reform agenda. Its full name is the Patient Protection and Affordable Care Act. The ACA is multifaceted, including enhanced enforcement provisions, expansion of Medicaid eligibility, and establishment of health insurance exchanges. It also prohibits health insurers from denying coverage based upon preexisting conditions.
AMA	A professional organization for physicians, also known as the American Medical Association. The AMA is the secretariat of the National Uniform Claim Committee, which has a formal consultative role under HIPAA. The AMA also maintains the current procedural terminology medical code set.
Ambulatory care	A term referring to all types of health services that do not require an overnight hospital stay.
American Hospital Association (AHA)	A healthcare industry association that represents the concerns of institutional providers. The AHA hosts the National Uniform Billing Committee, which has a formal consultative role under HIPAA.
Balance billing	When doctors or hospitals charge more than a payer-approved amount for the service received by a patient.
Benchmark	An identifiable indicator of superior performance by a medical care provider, which can be used as a reference to raise the mainstream of care for Medicare beneficiaries. The relative definition of "superior" will vary, but in many instances, a superior benchmark would be a provider that appears in the top 10% of all providers for more than one year for the specific indicator.
Beneficiary	A person who has health insurance through the Medicare or Medicaid program.

TERM	DEFINITION
Business associate (HIPAA)	A person or organization that performs a function or activity on behalf of a covered entity but is not part of the covered entity's workforce. A business associate can also be a covered entity in its own right. See also Part II, 45 *CFR* 160.103.
Case management	A process used by a doctor, nurse, or other health professional to manage a patient's healthcare. Case managers make sure that patients receive needed services and track patients' use of facilities and resources.
Case-mix index	The average DRG relative weight for all Medicare admissions.
Centers for Medicare & Medicaid Services (CMS)	The U.S. government agency responsible for administering Medicare, Medicaid, State Children's Health Insurance (SCHIP), HIPAA, CLIA, and other health-related programs.
Claim	A claim is a request for payment for services and benefits. Claims are also called "bills" for all Part A and Part B services billed through fiscal intermediaries. "Claim" is the word used for Part B physician/supplier services billed through the carrier. See also Medicare Part A; Medicare Part B.
Clinical Laboratory Improvement Amendments (CLIA)	CLIA provides oversight to certified laboratory entities and is implemented by the Division of Laboratory Services within the Survey and Certification Group under the Center for Clinical Standards and Quality.
Code of Federal Regulations	The official compilation of federal rules and requirements.
Code set	Under HIPAA, any set of codes used to encode data elements, such as tables of terms, medical concepts, medical diagnostic codes, or medical procedure codes. This includes both the codes and their descriptions. See also Part II, 45 *CFR* 162.103.
Coinsurance	The percent of the Medicare-approved amount that a beneficiary has to pay Part A and/or Part B. In the Original Medicare Plan, the coinsurance payment is a percentage of the approved amount for the service (such as 20%).
Confidentiality	A patient's right to talk with his or her healthcare provider without anyone else finding out what was said in the discussion.
Consent and authorization (HIPAA)	A covered entity may use or disclose personal health information only: • With the consent of the individual for treatment, payment, or healthcare operations • With the authorization of the individual for all other uses or disclosures • As permitted under this rule for certain public policy purposes
Consolidated Omnibus Budget Reconciliation Act (COBRA)	A law that requires an employer to allow for continuation of an individual's coverage under the employer's group health plan for a period of time after the individual experiences a death of his or her spouse, job loss, work hour reduction, or divorce. The individual may have to pay both his or her share and the employer's share of the premium. EMTALA was enacted as part of this law.
Contractor	An entity that has an agreement with CMS or another funding agency to perform a project.
Cost report	The report required from providers on an annual basis to make a proper determination of amounts payable under the Medicare program. The cost report should document the cost that the hospital incurred providing services. The amounts reported in cost reports are used by CMS to establish future payment increases.
Covered entity (HIPAA)	A health plan, healthcare clearinghouse, or healthcare provider that transmits any health information in electronic form in connection with a HIPAA transaction.

TERM	DEFINITION
Current Procedural Terminology (CPT®)	A medical code set of physician and other services, maintained and copyrighted by the American Medical Association (AMA) and adopted by the secretary of HHS as the standard for reporting physician and other services on standard transactions.
Deductible	The annual amount payable by a beneficiary for covered services before Medicare makes reimbursement.
Diagnosis code	The first of these codes is the ICD-10-CM diagnosis code describing the principal diagnosis (i.e., the condition established after study to be chiefly responsible for causing a hospitalization). The remaining codes are the ICD-10-CM diagnosis codes corresponding to additional conditions that coexisted at the time of admission or developed subsequently and that had an effect on the treatment received or the length of stay.
Discharge	The ending of an inpatient stay in a medical institution such as a hospital or a skilled nursing facility when continued retention of the patient would not meet medical necessity criteria.
Disclosure	Release or divulgence of information by an entity to persons or organizations outside of that entity.
Disproportionate share hospital	A hospital with a disproportionately large share of low-income patients. Under Medicaid, states augment payment to these hospitals. Medicare inpatient hospital payments also are adjusted for this added burden.
Downcode	To reduce the value and code of a claim when the documentation does not support the level of service billed by a provider.
DRG coding	The DRG categories used by hospitals on discharge billing. See also DRGs.
Diagnosis Related Groups (DRG)	A classification system that groups patients according to diagnosis, type of treatment, age, and other relevant criteria. Stands for "diagnosis-related groups." Under the prospective payment system, hospitals are paid a set fee for treating patients in a single DRG category, regardless of the actual cost of care for the individual.
Durable medical equipment (DME)	Equipment that serves primarily a medical purpose, is able to withstand repeated use, and is appropriate for use in the home; examples include wheelchairs, oxygen equipment, and hospital beds.
Durable medical equipment regional carrier	A private entity that contracts with Medicare to pay bills for DME.
Edit	Logic within the Standard Claims Processing System (or PSC Supplemental Edit Software) that selects certain claims, evaluates or compares information on the selected claims or other accessible source, and, depending on the evaluation, takes action on the claims, such as full payment, partial payment, or suspension for manual review.
Emergency Medical Treatment and Labor Act of 1986 (EMTALA)	EMTALA requires hospitals that have an emergency department to provide examination and stabilizing treatment for an emergency medical condition without consideration of insurance coverage or ability to pay.
Episode of care	The healthcare services given during a certain period of time, usually during a hospital stay.
Evaluation and management code	Codes used by physicians based on the resources they expended during the visit.

TERM	DEFINITION
Exclusions (Medicare)	Items or services that Medicare does not cover, such as most prescription drugs, long-term care, and custodial care in a nursing or private home.
Federal Register	The official daily publication for rules, proposed rules, and notices of federal agencies and organizations, as well as executive orders and other presidential documents. It is located at *www.federalregister.gov.*
Federally Qualified Health Center (FQHC)	Health centers located in medically underserved areas. FQHCs include community health centers, migrant health centers, and health centers for the homeless.
Fee schedule	A complete listing of fees used by health plans to pay doctors or other providers.
Fiscal year	For Medicare, a yearlong period that runs from October 1 to September 30 of the following year. The government and some insurance companies follow a budget that is planned for a fiscal year. Any organization may establish a fiscal year that is different from the government's fiscal year.
Form 1450	CMS' name for the institutional uniform claim form, or UB-92.
Form 1500	CMS' name for the professional uniform claim form, or UCF-1500.
Formulary	An approved list of certain drugs and their proper dosages. In some Medicare health plans, doctors must order or use only drugs listed on the health plan's formulary.
Fraud and abuse	Fraud: To bill purposely, and with knowledge, for services that were never given or were not medically necessary, or to bill for a service that has a higher reimbursement than the service performed. Abuse: Payment for items or services that are mistakenly billed by providers but should not be paid for by Medicare. Abuse is not the same as fraud.
Health Care Financing Administration	The former name of CMS.
Health Insurance Portability and Accountability Act of 1996 (HIPAA)	HIPAA provides protection for patients' protected health information to ensure that such information remains private and secure.
Healthcare Common Procedural Coding System (HCPCS)	A medical code set that identifies healthcare procedures, equipment, and supplies for claim submission purposes. It has been selected for use in the HIPAA transactions. HCPCS Level I contains numeric CPT codes, which are maintained by the AMA. HCPCS Level II contains alphanumeric codes used to identify various items and services that are not included in the CPT medical code set. These are maintained by CMS, the Blue Cross Blue Shield Association, and the Health Insurance Association of America. HCPCS Level III contains alphanumeric codes that are assigned by Medicaid state agencies to identify additional items and services not included in Levels I or II. These are usually called "local codes" and must have "W," "X," "Y," or "Z" in the first position. HCPCS procedure modifier codes can be used with all three levels, with the WA–ZY range used for locally assigned procedure modifiers.
High-risk area	A potential flaw in management controls requiring management attention and possible corrective action.
Home health agency	An organization that provides homecare services, such as skilled nursing care, physical therapy, occupational therapy, speech therapy, and care by home health aides.

TERM	DEFINITION
Hospice	Comprehensive care for people who are terminally ill; the care includes pain management, counseling, respite care, prescription drugs, inpatient care and outpatient care, and family services.
Hospital insurance (Part A)	The part of Medicare that pays for inpatient hospital stays, care in a skilled nursing facility, hospice care, and some home healthcare.
ICD and ICD-N-CM and ICD-N-PCS	International Classification of Diseases, with N = 10 for Revision 10, CM = Clinical Modification, and PCS = Procedure Coding System.
Incident to	Medicare Part B covers services rendered by employees of physicians or physician-directed clinics when the services provided are an integral, although incidental, part of the physician's personal professional services in the course of diagnosis or treatment of an injury or illness. To fulfill the requirements of this provision for services billable to the contractor, specific conditions must be met.
Inpatient	Medicare defines an inpatient as a patient who has been formally admitted into a hospital by a doctor.
Internal controls	Management systems and policies for reasonably documenting, monitoring, and correcting operational processes to prevent and detect waste and to ensure proper payment.
J codes	A subset of the HCPCS Level II code set with a high-order value of J that has been used to identify certain drugs and other items.
The Joint Commission	An organization that accredits healthcare organizations, formerly known as the Joint Commission on Accreditation of Healthcare Organizations, or JCAHO.
Lifetime reserve days	When a Medicare beneficiary is in the hospital for more than 90 days, Medicare pays for 60 additional reserve days that can be used only once in the beneficiary's lifetime. Reserve days cannot be renewed once they are used.
Medical insurance (Part B)	The part of Medicare that covers doctors' services and outpatient hospital care. It also covers other medical services that Part A does not cover, such as physical and occupational therapy.
Medically necessary	Services or supplies that are proper and needed for the diagnosis or treatment of a patient's medical condition; are provided for the diagnosis, direct care, and treatment of a patient's medical condition; meet the standards of good medical practice in the local area; and are not mainly for the convenience of a patient or the patient's doctor.
Medicare Administrative Contractor (MAC)	MACs are responsible for administering both Medicare Part A and Medicare Part B claims on behalf of CMS. MACs replaced Part A fiscal intermediaries and Part B carriers as of September 2013.
Modifier	Indicates that a service or procedure was altered by a specific circumstance that does not change the definition or code for that service or procedure.
Monitoring	A planned, systematic, and ongoing process to gather and organize data and to aggregate results in order to evaluate performance.
Noncovered service	A service that does not meet the requirements of a Medicare benefit category, is statutorily excluded from coverage on grounds other than 1862(a) (1), or is not reasonable and necessary under 1862(a)(1).
Nonphysician practitioner	Physician assistants, physical therapists, nurse practitioners, etc. May provide "incident to" services.

TERM	DEFINITION
Notice of proposed rulemaking	A document that describes and explains regulations that the federal government proposes to adopt at some future date and that invites interested parties to submit related comments. These comments can then be used in developing a final regulation.
Observation	Medicare defines observation services as an outpatient hospital stay in which an individual receives medical services to help the doctor decide whether the individual should be admitted to the hospital as an inpatient or discharged. Observation stays typically last no more than 24–48 hours.
Outlier	Additions to a full-episode payment in cases where costs of services delivered are estimated to exceed a fixed-loss threshold.
Part A (Medicare)	Hospital insurance that pays for inpatient hospital stays, care in a skilled nursing facility, hospice care, and some home healthcare.
Part B (Medicare)	Medical insurance that helps pay for doctors' services, outpatient hospital care, and other medical services that are not covered by Part A.
Part C (Medicare)	Medical insurance that is provided through a provider organization, such as an insurance entity. Medicare Part C is commonly referred to as "Medicare Advantage." Patients enrolling in Medicare Part C must have Medicare Parts A and B.
Part D (Medicare)	Prescription drug insurance that can be voluntarily purchased by a Medicare beneficiary.
Payer	In healthcare, an entity that assumes the risk of paying for medical treatments. This can be an uninsured patient, Medicare, Medicaid, Tricare, a self-insured employer, a health plan, or an HMO.
Postpayment review	The review of a claim after a determination and payment has been made to the provider or beneficiary.
Prospective payment system	A method of reimbursement in which Medicare payment is made based on a predetermined, fixed amount. The payment amount for a particular service is derived based on the classification system of that service (e.g., DRGs for inpatient hospital services).
Protected health information (HIPAA)	Individually identifiable health information transmitted or maintained in any form or medium, which is held by a covered entity or its business associate. This information identifies the individual or offers a reasonable basis for identification. It is created or received by a covered entity or an employer. Protected health information relates to a past, present, or future physical or mental condition, provision of healthcare, or payment for healthcare.
Quality	How well a health plan keeps its members healthy or treats them when they are sick. Good-quality healthcare means doing the right thing at the right time, in the right way, for the right person, and getting the best possible results.
Quality Improvement Organization (QIO)	A group of practicing doctors and other healthcare experts. QIOs are paid by the federal government to check and improve the care given to Medicare patients. They must review patients' complaints about the quality of care given by inpatient hospitals, hospital outpatient departments, hospital emergency rooms, skilled nursing facilities, home health agencies, private fee-for-service plans, and ambulatory surgical centers.
Referral	An "okay" from a patient's primary care doctor for the patient to see a specialist or get certain services. In many Medicare managed care plans, a patient must obtain a referral before receiving care from anyone except his or her primary care doctor. If a patient does not get a referral first, the plan may not pay for his or her care.

TERM	DEFINITION
Revenue code	Payment codes for services or items in FL 42 of the UB-92 found in Medicare/NUBC (National Uniform Billing Committee) manuals (42X, 43X, etc.).
Secondary payer	An insurance policy, plan, or program that pays second on a claim for medical care. This could be Medicare, Medicaid, or other health insurance, depending on the situation.
Skilled nursing facility	A Medicare-approved facility that provides short-term post-hospital extended care services at a lower level of care than provided in a hospital. A skilled nursing facility has staff and equipment to give skilled nursing care, skilled rehabilitation services, and other related health services.
Social Security Act	Public Law 74-271, enacted on August 14, 1935, with subsequent amendments. The Social Security Act consists of 20 titles, four of which have been repealed. The Health Insurance and Supplementary Health Insurance programs are authorized by Title XVIII of the Social Security Act.
Split/shared service	A patient encounter where the physician and a qualified nonphysician practitioner each personally perform a substantive portion of the service. The interaction with the patient must be face-to-face, and each must perform at least one of the following three components: history, examination, or medical decision-making. A split/shared evaluation and management encounter applies only in the following settings: hospital inpatient, hospital outpatient, hospital observation, emergency department, hospital discharge, office, and nonfacility clinic visits.
Supplier	Generally, any entity, person, or agency that gives a patient a medical item or service, like a wheelchair or walker.
Third-party administrator	An entity that is required to make or that is responsible for making payment on behalf of a group health plan.
Trading partner	External entity with whom business is conducted (i.e., customer). This relationship can be formalized via a trading partner agreement. (Note: A trading partner of an entity for some purposes may also be considered a business associate of that same entity for other purposes.)
Transaction	Under HIPAA, the exchange of information between two parties to carry out financial or administrative activities related to healthcare.
TRICARE	The Department of Defense's health insurance program for active duty and retired military personnel and their family members.
UB-92	An electronic format of the CMS-1450 paper claim form that has been in general use since 1993 for institutional services.